THE LAST RIDE

JOURNEY TO AUSCHWITZ-BIRKENAU

BY MANIT DANI

ISBN: 978-93-340-9736-8
Imprint: Independently published
Cover design by: Manit Dani

Email: manitdani@gmail.com
Instagram: <u>manitdani</u>

THIS BOOK IS DEDICATED TO MY FAMILY,
WHO TAUGHT
ME THE VALUE OF RELATIONSHIPS AND COMMUNITY.

In the shadow of Auschwitz's haunting history, we grapple with a profound philosophical puzzle that resonates through time. The tragic occurrences within these camp boundaries compel us to confront the darkest sides of human nature, challenging our understanding of morality, the absence of compassion, and the depths to which humanity can sink when faced with hatred. The camps function not just as reminders of past brutality but as a philosophical crucible, prompting reflections on the nature of free will and proving essential for preserving our shared humanity in the aftermath of such tragedy.

Since my journey to Berlin and other historic sites across Europe, I have been both fascinated and disturbed by large-scale crimes, many of which have occurred in my own country. My parents and grandparents, victims of the mass violence during the 1947 India-Pakistan partition, have made me especially sensitive to these stories. Visiting Auschwitz and Birkenau allowed me to see the remains of these atrocities firsthand. Although these sites witnessed genocide from 1940 to 1945, such horrors still exist in the world today.

As I undertake this exploration, the legacy of Auschwitz prompts me to contemplate the human condition and our collective dedication to justice, empathy, and the preservation of our humanity.

"What is done cannot be undone, but one can prevent it happening again".

- Anne Frank

Image captured by the author ©

This heartfelt photograph captures a stark display at Auschwitz 1, showing a historical image of the camp during winter. The scene within the frame depicts snow-covered ground dotted with the lifeless bodies of prisoners who did not live to see liberation. The bleak, frozen landscape underscores the harsh conditions and immense suffering endured by those interned at the camp. The rows of fence posts and the distant guard towers fade into the horizon, symbolising the extensive reach of the camp's oppression.

Image captured by the author ©

This evocative photograph, displayed at Auschwitz I, captures a moment inside one of the women's barracks shortly after liberation. The image shows a group of female prisoners sitting among the wooden bunks that were their living quarters. Their expressions range from weary resignation to cautious hope, reflecting the deep suffering they endured and the uncertain future they faced. The barracks, overcrowded and devoid of basic amenities, highlight the inhumane conditions under which these women lived.

Image captured by the author ©

This photograph captures an outdoor exhibit at Auschwitz 1, featuring a historical image of snow-covered train cars and the remnants of what appears to be a mass of abandoned belongings. It shows train cars that transported prisoners to Auschwitz, with the ground littered with personal items hastily discarded upon arrival. These items, once belonging to individuals who were torn from their homes and thrust into the horrors of the camp, symbolise the abrupt and violent interruption of countless lives. The snow adds a layer of starkness, emphasising the cold, harsh reality faced by those who were deported.

Image captured by the author ©

The photograph depicts an outdoor display at Auschwitz 1, showcasing historical images of the camp. A group of children is seen exiting barrack 2, their faces reflecting a mixture of fear and confusion. The harsh conditions they endured are evident in their expressions and the sparse, cold environment around them. Each child's gaze captures a moment of loss and the enduring impact of their suffering.

Prelude

In the depths of history lies a place that echoes with the silent screams of millions, where the shadows of the past dance with the light of remembrance. It invites the soul to go on a pilgrimage through understanding and compassion. This is the story of my journey to Auschwitz, a journey beyond mere physical travel, which delves into the heart of humanity's darkest hour.

In the records of human history, there are very few chapters in human history as harrowing and deeply unnerving as the Holocaust. The genocide, orchestrated by the Nazi regime during World War II left an indelible mark on the consciousness of humanity. Among the most horrifying sites of this unparalleled tragedy stands Auschwitz-Birkenau, a name synonymous with death and unimaginable suffering under a brutal dictatorship.

This book is aimed at exploring the harrowing narrative of Auschwitz-Birkenau, the place where the essence of human morality was torn apart. It is a journey into the darkest period of the 20th century, a period stained by the blood of innocent lives. According to research by historians like Franciszek Piper, whose studies were published by Yad Vashem and corroborated by institutions such as the United States Holocaust Memorial Museum and Auschwitz-Birkenau Museum, over 1.3 million individuals were sent to the camp, and over 1.1 million lost their lives there. Some historians even speculate that the number of deaths could have possibly reached as high as 1.5 million, encompassing not just Jews but also political prisoners, Romani people, and others deemed undesirable by the Nazi regime. This tragic reality underscores the industrial scale of death that Auschwitz represented, a factory of human annihilation that operated with efficiency. Through historical records, survivor testimonies, and the haunting remains of the camps, I aim to reveal the tragic events that occurred within its barbed wires.

The impetus behind this revelation stems from a deep sense of duty to honour the memories of those who suffered and perished. By delving into this painful chapter of history, my goal is to ensure that the horrors experienced by millions are never forgotten. It is crucial to educate current and future generations about these atrocities to foster a deep understanding of the consequences of hatred, bigotry, and indifference. The memory of Auschwitz is not just a relic of the past, it is a living warning, a perpetual reminder that the seeds of such cruelty can take root if left unchecked. The responsibility we bear is not only to remember but to actively work against the forces of intolerance in our own lives. As time moves forward, the obligation to keep these memories alive becomes even more crucial, ensuring that the lessons of Auschwitz continue to resonate across generations. In an age where the echoes of past horrors can so easily be drowned out by present distractions, it becomes all the more essential to keep these stories at the forefront of our collective consciousness. As I continue, it becomes a journey in someone else's thoughts, one of another time. What did make them hate so much? And how could a place like Auschwitz become a crucible of suffering for human beings? And perhaps most importantly, what lessons are there to be learned from the shadows of Auschwitz for us to protect our humanity?

This is not merely an unfolding of historical events but a sincere attempt to pay respect to the millions who suffered, were murdered, and struggled within its grip. It is a tribute to the strength of the human spirit and an appeal not to forget horrors of the past, so they are never repeated. In the pages that follow, we confront the legacy of Auschwitz, acknowledging its significance as a warning against the potential consequences of intolerance and hate. In other words, my reasons to visit Auschwitz were deeply rooted in a personal understanding of its historical, humanistic, and moral importance. It was a pilgrimage driven by a commitment to understanding and an enduring obligation to honour the memory of the past. This is not just a book of history but a clarion call toward remembering, reflecting, and acting for the sake of human dignity.

May this exploration serve as a testament to the enduring need for affinity and compassion in the face of unspeakable tragedy. And so, with that heavy heart but inspired spirit, I will go forth to my first steps toward Auschwitz with the light of remembrance and hope for a better tomorrow. Through each word, through every page, let us never forget and always work toward the goal of making a world in which such evil activities can never again be allowed to take root. In all of us, the stories of Auschwitz should ignite a sense of responsibility against tyranny, fostering a commitment to uphold values of compassion, justice, and humanity in our everyday lives. By embracing this commitment, we ensure that the sacrifices of the past pave the way for a future where such darkness can never take hold again. Let this journey be a beacon of hope, a testament to the resilience of the human spirit, and a clarion call to ensure that the lessons of the past guide us towards a more humane and just future.

CONTENTS

Chapter 1: Introduction

Chapter 2: Crossing the Threshold

Chapter 3: Behind the Barbed Wire

Chapter 4: Faces in Photographs

Chapter 5: Walking Through History

Chapter 6: Birkenau's Vastness

Chapter 7: The Remains of Crematoria

Chapter 8: Stories of Survival and Resistance

Chapter 9: After the War

Chapter 10: The Role of Remembrance

Chapter 11: Lessons for Today

Conclusion: Echoes that Endure

Image captured by the author ©

This photograph captures the iconic entrance to Auschwitz II-Birkenau, known as the "Gate of Death," through which the railway tracks extend into the camp. The perspective of the tracks, leading the viewer's eye directly to the gate, evokes a sense of the countless journeys that ended here. Under a vast, cloudy sky, the imposing structure stands as a reminder of the industrial-scale Genocide that took place here.

CHAPTER 1
INTRODUCTION

A decision to visit Auschwitz was made for countless reasons, each stemming from a deep sense of historical curiosity, a yearning for understanding, and a profound respect for the significance of this place. Despite my desire to visit, I hesitated for years. The thought of witnessing the horrors of the Holocaust filled me with a sense of nervousness, a fear of diving into the depths of human depravity. Moreover, the logistical challenges and the emotional toll of such a journey were significant, deterring me from taking the leap.

But as the years passed, the pull of Auschwitz only grew stronger. It became clear this was a journey I could not postpone indefinitely. The lessons to be learned from Auschwitz were too significant to ignore. With a mixture of anticipation and apprehension, I resolved to finally make the pilgrimage. This decision was not merely driven by a desire to witness a historical site, but was rooted in a deeply personal quest for knowledge and remembrance. First and foremost, the significance of Auschwitz as a pivotal site of the Holocaust was a compelling factor driving my desire to visit. I recognised the unparalleled importance of bearing witness to a place that stands as a strong testament to the darkest chapter of human existence.

The magnitude of the suffering, the resilience of the human spirit, and the enduring legacy of the Holocaust made Auschwitz a site of historical significance that I felt compelled to experience firsthand. Moreover, my visit to Auschwitz was driven by a serious yearning to pay homage to the victims of the Holocaust. The names and faces of those who perished in the concentration camps had become more than mere historical statistics. They had become symbols of the immeasurable loss and the relentless spirit of those who had endured unimaginable horrors. I felt a responsibility to honour their memory, to stand in solidarity with their legacy, and to ensure that their stories would not be consigned to the annals of history.

The broader historical background leading up to the establishment of Auschwitz is crucial for understanding its role within the larger framework of the Holocaust, also sometimes referred to as "the Shoah," the Hebrew word for "catastrophe." The rise of the Nazi Party in Germany, with its ideology centred on Aryan supremacy and antisemitism, set the stage for the systemic persecution of Jews and other minority groups. The Nazis wrongfully accused Jews of being responsible for Germany's social, economic, political, and cultural issues. They particularly held them accountable for Germany's defeat in World War I (1914-1918). This scapegoating found a receptive audience among some Germans. The collective anger over the war's loss, coupled with the subsequent economic and political crises, fueled the rise of antisemitism in German society. Also, the instability during the Weimar Republic (1918-1933), the looming threat of communism, and the devastating economic impact of the Great Depression further inclined many Germans towards Nazi ideology, including its antisemitic components.

Following Adolf Hitler's ascent to power in 1933, as the leader of the National Socialist German Worker's Party (NSDAP), more commonly known as the Nazi Party, antisemitic laws and policies gradually stripped Jews of their rights and freedoms, culminating in the outbreak of World War II and the implementation of *The Final Solution*, a plan to exterminate the Jewish population of Europe.

However, the Nazis did not invent antisemitism. Antisemitism, an entrenched and widespread prejudice, long predates the Nazis. In Europe, it has ancient roots. During the Middle Ages, biases against Jews were largely driven by early Christian beliefs, especially the false accusation that Jews were responsible for the death of Jesus. These religious prejudices persisted into early modern Europe till 1800s, where Jewish communities were often isolated from economic, social, and political life by Christian leaders. This exclusion fostered stereotypes that painted Jews as perpetual outsiders.

As Europe became more secular, many places lifted most legal restrictions on Jews. However, this did not mark the end of antisemitism. In the 18th and 19th centuries, new forms of antisemitism emerged, including economic, nationalist, and racial antisemitism. During the 19th century, antisemites falsely accused Jews of causing numerous social and political problems in modern, industrial society. Pseudoscientific theories of race, eugenics, and Social Darwinism were used to justify these hatreds. Nazi prejudice against Jews drew on all these elements, particularly racial antisemitism, which is the discriminatory belief that Jews constitute a separate and inferior race. The Nazis believed that world was divided into distinct races, with some inherently superior to others. They regarded Germans as part of the supposedly superior "Aryan" race. Furthermore, the Nazis viewed the "Jewish race" as inferior and dangerous. They perceived Jews as a threat that needed to be eradicated from German society. The Nazis insisted that if not removed, the "Jewish race" would corrupt and ultimately destroy the German people.

In the spring of 1940, Heinrich Himmler, the Reichsführer-SS, commanded a group of prisoners to construct a camp in Oswiecim, a small town in upper Silesia. Auschwitz, as it was named in German, was chosen for several strategic reasons. One of the primary factors was its location. Situated in the heart of Nazi-occupied Poland, Auschwitz was centrally located within Europe, making it an ideal hub for the transport of Jews and other prisoners from various parts of the continent. The town of Oswiecim was also well-connected by rail, with extensive railway lines that allowed for the efficient and easy transportation of large numbers of prisoners to the camp. Additionally, the area around Auschwitz was sparsely populated, which allowed the Nazis to operate the camp with a certain degree of secrecy, away from the prying eyes of the international community. The region's industrial resources were also significant, as the Nazis sought to exploit the forced labor of prisoners in nearby factories, including the IG Farben plant, which produced synthetic rubber and other war materials. Furthermore, Auschwitz had previously served as a Polish military base, which meant that some barracks were already in place, providing a ready-made infrastructure for the Nazis to expand upon. This existing military infrastructure allowed for a quicker and more efficient establishment of the camp, enabling the rapid scaling up of operations. This made Auschwitz, an optimal location for the Nazis to carry out their genocidal objectives.

However, the journey to Auschwitz for many Jews began long before 1940, in the overcrowded and brutal ghettos established by the Nazis. Before the mass deportations to concentration and extermination camps, Jews were forcibly confined to ghettos, which were walled-off sections of cities where they lived in squalid, inhumane conditions. These ghettos were not merely holding areas but were intended to isolate, control, and degrade the Jewish population. Life in the ghettos was marked by extreme deprivation. The Nazi authorities deliberately restricted access to food and medical supplies, leading to rampant malnutrition and the spread of deadly diseases like typhus. Despite these dire circumstances, Jewish communities struggled to preserve their humanity by establishing underground schools, religious services, and cultural activities. The Krakow Ghetto, located very near to Auschwitz, became one of the sites of unimaginable suffering and violence claiming countless lives. Ghettos served as cruel waiting rooms, where the Jewish population, stripped of their rights and dignity, awaited the inevitable transport to camps like Auschwitz.

The establishment of Auschwitz was part of a broader strategy to utilize forced labor for the German war effort while systematically exterminating those deemed undesirable by the Nazi regime (which called itself the Third Reich). Tragically, over 1.3 million people lost their lives here, with more than ninety percent being of Jewish descent. Beyond the historical and humanistic significance, I sought to visit Auschwitz as a means of confronting the uncomfortable truths of the past. As the date of departure drew nearer, countless thoughts and feelings churned within, shaping the mind to this journey into the heart of darkness. The visit demanded a level of emotional strength and introspection that could not be rushed. It was a journey that necessitated a thorough internal reckoning with the magnitude of the Holocaust's horrors and a sober acknowledgment of the emotional impact such an experience would inevitably involve.

The idea of visiting Auschwitz grew over years of reading, studying, and anticipating the Holocaust, an event that shook the world. One moment that solidified my decision to visit Auschwitz occurred when I visited Holocaust Museums. Seeing and listening to survivors recount their harrowing experiences, the loss of families, and the unimaginable suffering they endured, I was moved to tears. Their stories transformed my abstract understanding of the Holocaust into a personal connection, making the journey to Auschwitz feel not only necessary but urgent.

Moreover, I got influenced by reading Elie Wiesel's "Night." His vivid and powerful portrayal of life in the concentration camps, his struggles with faith and survival, and his reflections on humanity and inhumanity left an indelible mark on my soul. The book was more than a recounting of events, it was a powerful testament to the strength of the human spirit and a call to remember and learn from the past. The stories of survivors, the touching images, and the sheer magnitude of the massacres had left a mark on my consciousness, demanding many answers. The personal motivations were tangled with a desire for a connection. It was a search to understand the incomprehensible, to touch the tangible remains of a history that had shaped the world. The names and faces of those who had perished were no longer unknown, they became part of me, pleading for recognition and remembrance.

I was fueled by a sense of responsibility, a responsibility to the past and a commitment to ensuring that the lessons learned from the horrors of the Holocaust would not fade into silence. It was a recognition that these stories were not relics of a bygone era but are part of our lives today. To understand Auschwitz, one had to dig into the historical context that gave rise to it. The camp, situated in the heart of Nazi-occupied Poland, became the epicentre of a Genocidal campaign, *The Final Solution*. It wasn't merely a concentration camp, it was a symbol of dehumanisation and industrialised murder.

No other word conjures the terrors of the Holocaust quite like the name Auschwitz. This immense complex stood as the largest of the Nazi concentration camps, where millions met their tragic end, falling victim to gas, beatings, shootings, illness, medical experiments, and the harsh realities of exhaustion and starvation. Notable figures such as Rudolf Höss, the camp's first commandant, played pivotal roles in the efficient and brutal operations of Auschwitz. Höss oversaw the implementation of mass murder techniques, including the use of Zyklon B gas in the chambers. Prisoners from Western, Central, and Eastern Europe were forcibly transported to this labor and death camp, located approximately 56 km from the Polish city of Kraków. Regrettably, the majority of them would never return. The initial completion of the main camp, Auschwitz I, took place in June 1940. It was succeeded by Auschwitz II (Birkenau), explicitly designed as a death camp, and then Auschwitz III, or Buna-Monowitz, the largest forced labor camp within the Auschwitz complex. Subsequently, numerous smaller camps, labor facilities, and factories emerged around these central hubs. Each day, packed cattle-cars arrived, transporting Jewish and non-Jewish prisoners from all corners of Nazi occupied Europe. Upon arrival, they underwent the infamous selection process, sending the majority, including children, pregnant women, the elderly, and the deemed 'unfit,' to gas chambers and cremation. Those who survived the selections were distributed among the Auschwitz camps, where, in most cases, they succumbed to starvation, overwork or disease. When the Red Army liberated the camp on January 27th 1945, they encountered only 7,500 sickly survivors, the remnant of the tens of thousands forced on death marches to Germany through the harsh winter. Auschwitz's significance lay not just in its physical dimensions but in the ugly reality that unfolded within its fences. It was a place where humanity faced its darkest reflection. A mirror reflecting the capacity for cruelty, hatred, and indifference. The historical weight of Auschwitz was a burden carried not only by the bricks and the wires but also by the morals of humanity. This journey therefore, became a journey through time. A period stained with the blood of innocent people. The impact was not confined to the past, it resonated through the present, urging acknowledgment of the murders and a commitment to prevent their recurrence.

As the departure date approached, my expectations mingled with apprehension. The prospect of standing on the very ground that witnessed the suffering, raised a mixture of emotions, wonder, fear and curiosity. The mind was occupied with conflicting sentiments, torn between the eagerness to understand and the fear of uncovering the darkness. Yet, the anticipation was a signal, drawing one closer to an understanding that surpassed photos, textbooks and documentaries seen. The journey to Auschwitz had begun, not merely as a physical voyage, but as an exploration of the soul, a journey into the heart of humanity's capacity for both darkness and light.

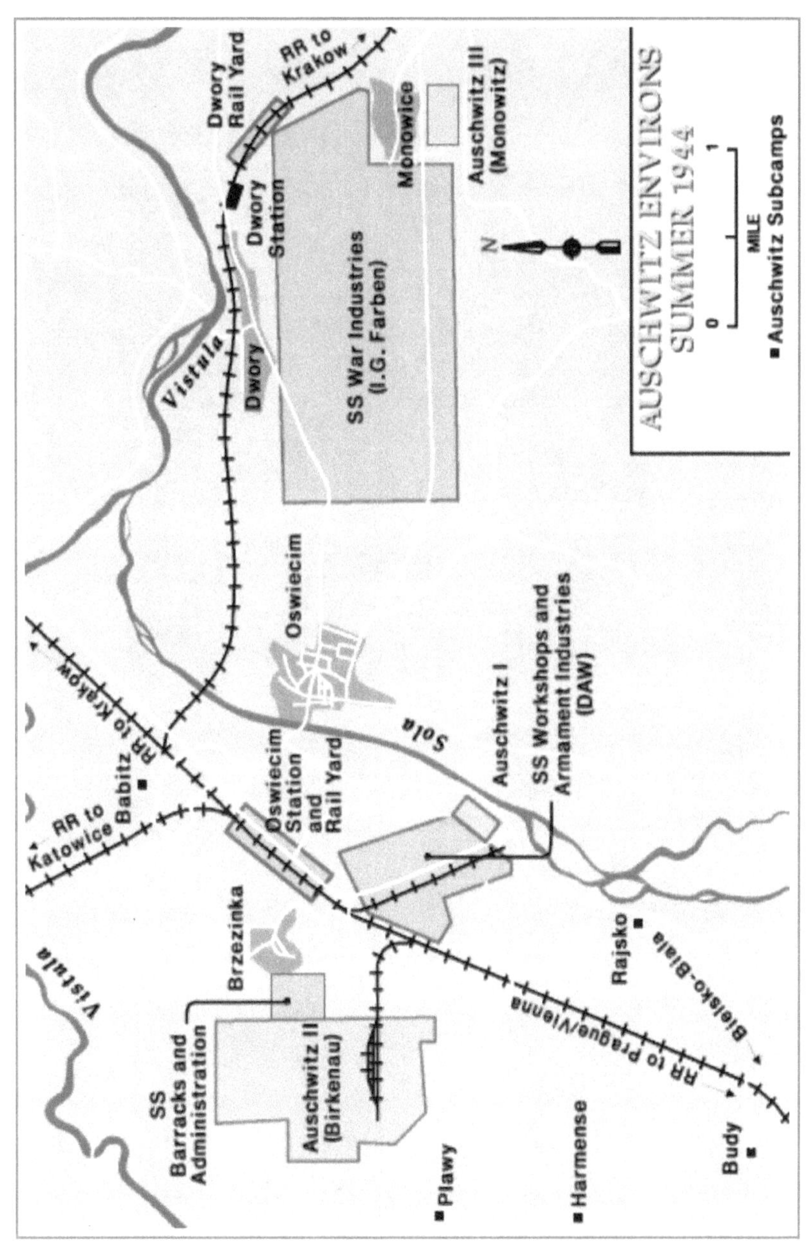

Auschwitz Territory, Summer 1944.
Source: United States Holocaust Memorial Museum.

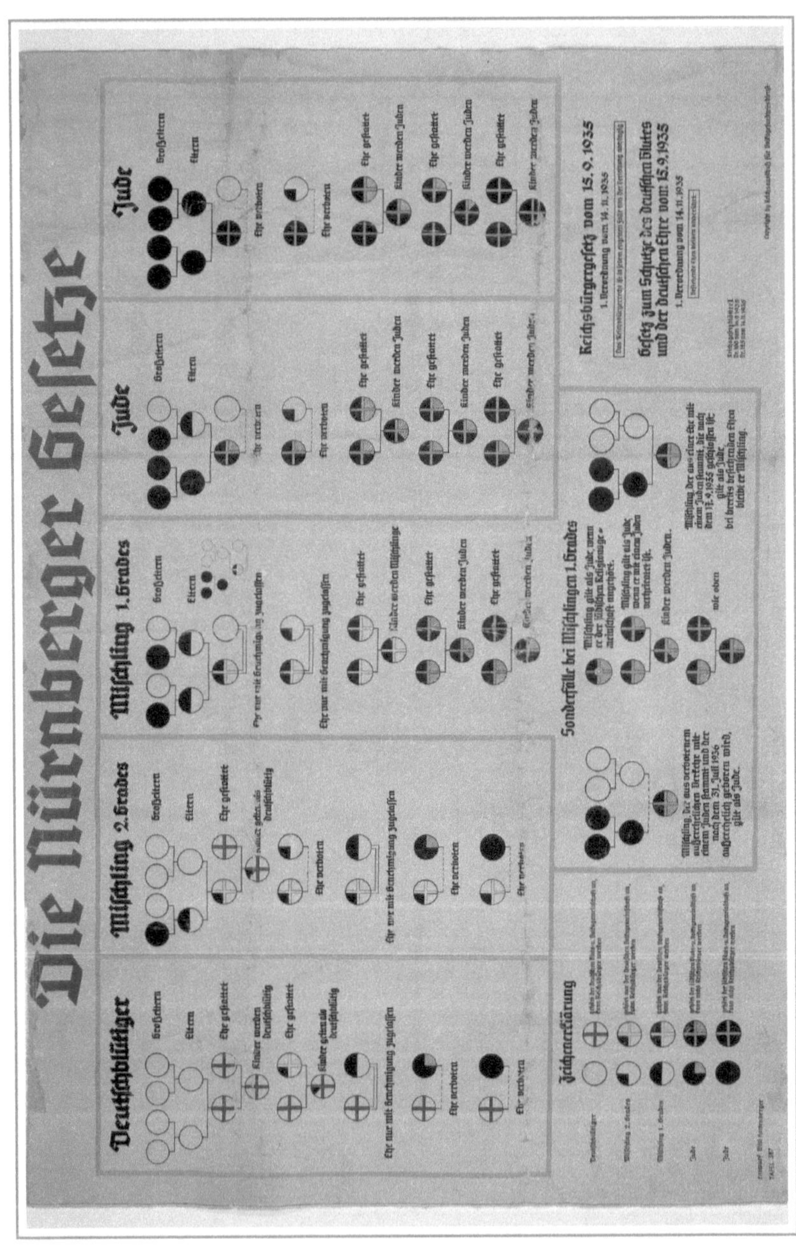

Chart explaining the racial classifications established by the Nuremberg Laws of 1935, used by the Nazis to enforce antisemitic policies.

Source: United States Holocaust Memorial Museum.

The Nuremberg Laws, introduced by the Nazi regime in 1935, marked a pivotal moment in the systematic persecution of Jews in Germany. These laws, rooted in deeply ingrained anti-Semitic ideology, provided a legal framework for the marginalisation and eventual annihilation of the Jewish people. The chart shown in the image is a visual representation of the racial classification system implemented under these laws, which reduced human beings to mere fractions of "Jewish blood" and determined their fate based on ancestry.

The chart outlines the categories defined by the Nazis to classify individuals according to their racial purity. At the top of the chart are full black circles, representing individuals with four Jewish grandparents. These people were automatically classified as Jews under Nazi law, irrespective of their religious beliefs or self-identification. This rigid classification meant that their lives were subject to the full extent of the Nazi regime's anti-Semitic policies, including segregation, forced labor, and eventual deportation to concentration and extermination camps like Auschwitz. The laws also introduced the concept of "Mischlings," a derogatory term used to describe individuals of mixed Jewish and non-Jewish ancestry. First-degree Mischlings, depicted by half-black circles, were those with two Jewish grandparents. Second-degree Mischlings, represented by quarter-black circles, had one Jewish grandparent. Although Mischlings were not fully classified as Jews, they still faced significant restrictions and discrimination. They were barred from certain professions, subjected to social ostracism, and, in many cases, later reclassified as Jewish based on other criteria or personal decisions by Nazi officials.

Conversely, full white circles on the chart symbolize individuals with four non-Jewish grandparents, classified as "Aryan" by the Nazis. Those labeled as Aryan were considered racially pure and were afforded full citizenship and the privileges that came with being part of the so-called "master race." This classification was central to Nazi racial ideology, which sought to preserve the purity of the Aryan race while systematically excluding, marginalising, and ultimately exterminating those deemed racially inferior. By reducing complex human identities to simplistic racial fractions, the Nazis stripped individuals of their dignity and humanity. These classifications determined who could marry, who could hold certain jobs, and, most chillingly, who would live or die. The Nuremberg Laws laid the groundwork for the Holocaust by legally codifying racial discrimination and setting the stage for the mass deportations and exterminations that would follow. It underscores the terrifying power of ideology when coupled with state machinery, demonstrating how the systematic categorization of people can lead to their total destruction.

Image captured by the author ©

This photograph shows a fragment of the Kraków Ghetto wall in Poland, built by the Nazis in 1941 to isolate the Jewish population. The wall's tombstone-like design symbolizes the tragic fate of the Jews who suffered and died during the Holocaust. The plaque memorializes those imprisoned within this boundary . Today, this wall fragment stands as a powerful symbol of remembrance and Holocaust education.

Image captured by the author ©

The Nazis deported about 2,32,000 children and young people to Auschwitz, including 2,16,000 jewish children, 11,000 Roma (Gypsy) children, 3,000 Polish children and 1,000 Slavic children of other nationalities. The Majority of the jewish children perished in the gas chambers immediately after arrival. Altogether about 22,000 children and young people of various nationalities were registered as prisoners. On 27th January 1945, Red Army soldiers liberated about 650 children and young people, of which 450 were under 15 years old in the camp.

Image captured by the author ©

This photograph captures the infamous entrance gate of Auschwitz I, bearing the deceptive inscription "Arbeit Macht Frei," which translates to "Work sets you free." The gate looms beneath a barren tree, symbolising the grim reality that awaited those who passed through. The wet, uneven path reflects the somber atmosphere, while a few visitors walk down the desolate street. This image illustrates the cruel irony and the false hope that the gate represented to millions of innocent lives.

CHAPTER 2
CROSSING THE THRESHOLD

In the quiet hours before dawn, as the world slumbers under a blanket of darkness, there exists a threshold marking the beginning of a journey both physical and spiritual. My heart was pounding, a mix of anxiety and anticipation swirling within me as I prepared to step into one of history's most distressing periods. This threshold beckons the traveler to step beyond the familiar confines of the everyday world and into the realm of history, memory, and remembrance. I felt a knot in my stomach, wondering if I was ready to face the reality of what had happened here. This is the story of crossing the path to Auschwitz, a journey that defies time and space, inviting introspection and understanding. With a sense of purpose and determination, I took that first step forward, crossing into the unknown.

The air was heavy with anticipation as I stood on the threshold of history, my heart filled with a mixture of anxiety and desire. For years, the idea of visiting Auschwitz had lingered in my mind, calling with a sense of urgency and purpose. But it wasn't until now, at this moment, that I felt ready to embark on the journey of a lifetime. My desire to visit Auschwitz was born from a deep-seated need to bear witness and pay homage to the millions of lives lost in the depths of human depravity. Growing up, I was captivated by stories of persistence and survival in the face of unimaginable adversity. These tales left an indelible mark on my consciousness, igniting a fervent desire to learn more, to understand, and to remember.

As I approached Auschwitz, I could hear the crunch of gravel under my feet and the distant murmur of other visitors. The air was thick with a musty smell, a mixture of damp earth and aged wood, adding to the atmosphere of solemnity. Stepping into the camp was a surreal and deeply emotional experience for me. Approaching the gates of Auschwitz, a biting coldness and mild rain added to the sorrows that hung heavily in the air. The weather, with its grey sky casting a dark shade over the landscape, reflected the sincerity of the moment. It seemed to mirror the solemn atmosphere that enveloped the camp. Despite the discomfort, I felt a sense of solemnity settle over me, amplified by the barren surroundings. The chilling cold seemed to deter many visitors, resulting in a surprisingly less crowd. The absence of bustling footsteps and murmured conversations only heightened the silence in the air. It was as though the weather itself mourned the tragic history. Standing at the gates of this place, it became apparent that Auschwitz wasn't just a location on the map, it was deeply etched in the collective consciousness of humanity. A solemn ground that bore witness to the most tragic episodes of our history.

An intense stillness surrounded me as I proceeded. The vastness of the site before my eyes was a silent witness to the magnitude of the human tragedy that had unfolded here. The first impression was not just visual, it was an instinctive feeling that resonated through my whole body. Each step felt like an intrusion, as if I were trespassing on hallowed ground. The brick barracks, standing in orderly rows, seemed to echo with the ghosts of the past. Each step on the gravel pathways carried the weight of the people who had walked the same ground, their destinies forever changed by the brutal regime.

I paused for a moment, closed my eyes, and tried to imagine the cacophony of sounds that once filled this space with the clatter of boots, the shouts of commands, and the cries of the suffering. The atmosphere was charged with an energy that redefined time. A reminder to all that history was not confined to textbooks but rang through the very air one breathed. Passing under the gate known as "Gate of Death" with the inscription, *"Arbeit Macht Frei,"* a shiver ran down my spine, The phrase, a German expression that translates to *"Work sets you free,"* has its roots in an 1873 novel written by Lorenz Diefenbach. The sign was created by the camp's ironworker and installed by the prisoners. In defiance of the slogan, they flipped the letter "B" upside down. It has been said that there was also a sarcastic rhyme about the slogan: *"Arbeit macht frei durch Krematorium Nummer drei,"* meaning *"Work will set you free through crematory number three."*

This infamous sign, made from cold, unyielding iron, bore witness to the suffering and death of countless individuals. Its powerful symbolism did not end with the war. In December 2009, the sign was stolen from its place above the entrance gate, shocking the world. The theft of such a significant artifact was more than just an act of vandalism, it was an affront to the memory of those who perished at Auschwitz. The sign was eventually recovered, cut into three pieces by the thieves, who intended to sell it on the black market. The recovery of the sign highlighted its significance as a symbol of the Holocaust, and its return was a reminder of the ongoing responsibility to preserve the memory of the atrocities committed here.

However, the irony is, the promise of freedom through labor was in conflict with the false hopes given to all. It wasn't merely a gate, it was a portal into a world of deception, where the thin layer of hope covered the ugly reality that awaited those who crossed it. The gate and its sign were made as a cruel psychological tool by the Nazis to mislead prisoners into believing that hard work could lead to their release, masking the brutal reality of their fates. It served to manipulate and control, embedding a false sense of hope that only deepened the despair within the camp.

The gate, more than a physical barrier, became a symbol of the manipulation and cruelty that described the camp. The words carved in iron had a strong impact that went beyond the script. They were a dark reminder that seemingly harmless ideas could be twisted in the service of oppression. Crossing into the gates of Auschwitz was not just a physical act, it was a step into history. The memories of the past sat on my shoulders like an invisible burden, and the air itself seemed filled with the sorrow of the millions who had suffered and perished within these walls. It was a moment of reckoning recognition, acknowledging that I stood on this sacred ground.

As I walked deeper into Auschwitz, I noticed specific details that made the horror palpable. The barracks, with their narrow bunks stacked three high, each space too small for a person to sit up fully, seemed to whisper the stories of countless nights of suffering. The initial impressions remained within, leaving a mark on my consciousness as Auschwitz was not just a physical place, it was a symbol of the depths of human cruelty and the capacity for evil. The rusted barbed wire, once a barrier to freedom, now stood as a reminder of the atrocities committed in the name of hatred. I recalled a story I had read about a young girl, no older than fourteen, who had kept a diary during her time here. Her entries, filled with fear, hope, and the longing for freedom, gave a face to the countless victims.

The threshold had been crossed, not just in space but also in time. Real incidents with Holocaust survivors unfolded, a testament to resilience, courage, and the enduring human spirit amidst the solemn echoes of history. My journey had just begun, and already, the impact of Auschwitz was searing itself into my very soul.

Entrance to the main camp of Auschwitz (Auschwitz I). The gate bears the motto "Arbeit Macht Frei" (Work makes one free).
Source - United States Holocaust Memorial Museum, courtesy of Instytut Pamieci Narodowej

Image captured by Mateus Campos Felipe Published on July 16, 2019

This photograph captures a guard tower and warning sign at Auschwitz 1. The guard tower, with its distinct sloped roof and multiple windows, was a vantage point used by Nazi guards to oversee the camp and monitor the prisoners. In the foreground, the "Halt! Stoj!" sign, adorned with a skull and crossbones, is a chilling warning. This bilingual sign, in German and Polish, translates to "Stop!" and was intended to deter prisoners from attempting to escape, under threat of immediate execution by guards stationed in the towers or patrolling the perimeter.

Page 33

Image captured by Karsten Winegeart Published on September 16, 2020

This photograph shows one of the many pathways between the brick barracks at Auschwitz I. On either side of the path are the brick buildings that housed prisoners in cramped and inhumane conditions. These barracks were originally constructed as Polish military barracks before being converted into prison blocks by the Nazis. The barbed-wire fences, equipped with electric wiring, ensured that escape was nearly impossible here. This image powerfully conveys the moving legacy of Auschwitz and the enduring memory of its victims.

This photograph captures Auschwitz 1. The remnants of barbed wire fences and guard towers are visible, highlighting the camp's extensive security measures designed to prevent any escape attempts. The solitary tree in the centre of the photograph stands as a silent witness to the horrors that occurred here. It evokes a sense of mourning and reflection, symbolising both the endurance of nature and the memory of the countless lives lost.

CHAPTER 3
BEHIND THE BARBED WIRE

Auschwitz, with its sprawling expanse of barbed wire fences and crumbling barracks, represented the epicentre of this tragic chapter in history. It was a place where innocence was extinguished in the flames of hatred and discrimination. Walking through the camp, each step drew me further into the heart of pain and despair. The red-bricked barracks and barbed wire bore witness to the suffering of countless souls. As I went on, I couldn't help but be overwhelmed by a sense of fear and sorrow. Seeing the barracks and barbed wire for the first time was like a punch to the gut. The sight of these symbols of imprisonment and oppression stirred a sense of grief and anger within me. Each barbed wire strand seemed to whisper the agonies of those who had once been held behind them, their dreams and futures cruelly extinguished.

As I stepped closer, the sight of the barbed wire fences was etched against the sky, sent a chill through me . It was   once a symbol of imprisonment and oppression, now it stands as a sentinel guarding the memories of the millions who died within its boundaries. They stood as silent sentinels, bearing witness to the unfathomable suffering and despair that unfolded within this place. The sharp, twisted wires seemed to stretch endlessly, each one a cruel reminder of the boundaries that had kept hope and humanity confined. Behind the barbed wire lay a world shrouded in darkness, a world where humanity's most heinous crimes were perpetrated against the innocent. This place unfolded itself as a sobering image of history. The barracks, standing in rows, seemed to close in around me as I walked the pathways that countless prisoners had lived in before. The oppressive presence of the barracks, once filled with the voices and movements of countless souls, now stood silent, their walls held within them the untold stories and unending pain. The surroundings amplified the gravity of the killings committed within these walls, and the very ground beneath my feet seemed to whisper the stories of those who had suffered.

The faint sound of gravel crunching underfoot and the occasional rustle of leaves in the wind added to the eerie silence. The smell of damp earth and aged wood filled the air, mingling with the faint scent of decay. The architectural layout of Auschwitz served as a reminder of the calculated precision that characterised the Nazi regime's machinery of death. Each building, each structure, was a gear in the merciless apparatus. Standing before these barracks, I couldn't help but reflect on the sheer evil of turning such precise organisation towards the goal of mass murder. It was a chilling reminder of how ordinary structures could be twisted into instruments of unimaginable cruelty. As I explored the camp, the more curious I became.

I learned that Auschwitz was comprised of 22 brick structures, with eight of them being two-story buildings. Additional floors were added to the remaining structures in 1943, along with another eight blocks. These expansions were driven by the Nazi's insatiable demand to house more prisoners, as the camp evolved from a place of forced labor into one of extermination. Stepping inside the barrack, I was immediately struck by the contrast between the intense cold environment and the harsh living conditions that prisoners had to face. The barracks felt like tombs, devoid of warmth and filled with the echoes of past horrors. The cold seemed to seep into my bones, mirroring the chilling reality of life and death within these walls. The overcrowded quarters, with their wooden bunk beds and insufficient belongings, offered a glimpse of an existence that became a daily struggle for survival. It was hard to fathom how so many had been forced to live in such dire conditions, their humanity stripped away bit by bit by the relentless cruelty of their captors.

The barracks of Auschwitz were designed to hold a specific number of prisoners, but the actual truth is that these numbers were often exceeded. Originally planned to accommodate around 700 inmates, the reality often saw up to 1,200 individuals crammed into a single barrack. The overcrowded conditions exacerbated the already dire circumstances, creating an environment where personal space and dignity became distant memories. Inside these structures, prisoners were greeted by wooden bunk beds, offering minimal respite from the relentless hardships. These bunks, often three tiers high, were nothing more than rough planks of wood, sometimes shared by multiple people. There were no mattresses, only thin straw sacks, often infested with lice, that provided little comfort against the hard wood. The prisoners, already weakened by starvation, forced labor, and brutality, were expected to sleep in these cramped, cold, and filthy conditions. Rest was nearly impossible, as the constant noise, the crying of the sick, and the pervasive fear of what the next day might bring kept many awake through the long, freezing nights.

Belongings were scarce, and personal items were a luxury seldom afforded. Many prisoners arrived at Auschwitz with the few possessions they could carry, only to have them confiscated upon arrival. What remained were often just the clothes on their backs, which quickly became tattered and inadequate against the harsh Polish winters. The sight of those wooden bunks, stacked like sardine cans, was a stark testament to the dehumanisation faced by the prisoners. Each bunk represented not just a place to sleep, but a tiny corner of hope and despair. A place where one might huddle for warmth with fellow prisoners, share whispered conversations, or shed silent tears. The lack of privacy and the constant proximity to others intensified the struggle for basic human comfort. The overcrowded conditions were not just a byproduct of inefficiency or indifference, they were a deliberate tactic to crush the spirit, to strip away individuality, and to reduce human beings to mere numbers in a machine of death.

Auschwitz became a convergence point for individuals from diverse nationalities, each carrying a unique story of tragedy. Prisoners came from countries all across Europe, including Poland, Hungary, France, Netherlands, Greece, Czechoslovakia, Belgium, Yugoslavia, Italy, Norway, and Germany, among others. The walls of the barracks resonated with the languages of Europe, capturing the essence of a continent torn apart by war. The amalgamation of cultures within these confines showcased the indiscriminate reach of the Holocaust. The food rations provided to prisoners further epitomised the brutality of their existence. In the morning, inmates received a meager portion of coffee or a thin, watery broth masquerading as soup. Lunch typically consisted of a small portion of watery soup made from rotten vegetables, often turnips, or sometimes even just nettles and grass. Dinner was no better, usually consisting of a small piece of bread, often stale and barely edible sometimes accompanied by a tiny piece of margarine, a slice of sausage, or a spoonful of marmalade. The thought of such meager rations being the only sustenance for these individuals was heart-wrenching, a contrast to the abundance many of us take for granted. During mealtimes, the air would be filled with a sense of desperation as inmates received scant portions, hardly sufficient to sustain life. The struggle for survival extended beyond the barbed wire, becoming an agonising daily reality within the barracks. Sanitation facilities were rudimentary, adding another layer of despair to the prisoners' daily lives. Shared toilets and bathing areas, with minimal provisions, underscored the dehumanising conditions within the barracks. The lack of basic hygiene was not just a physical hardship, but a psychological one, further stripping away the dignity of those imprisoned here. Hygiene became a luxury, and disease loomed as a constant threat.

As I walked through the reconstructed barracks, I started to imagine the pictures of the prisoners with overcrowded conditions, the lack of privacy, and the constant threat of disease, hunger, and violence. It was an emotional shock. Each step I took, was burdened by their suffering, each corner a reminder of the unimaginable hardships they faced. It was not just about the physical spaces but a journey into the psychological trauma that accompanied their lives within the barbed wire. The unforgettable visuals of history played out before my eyes, the personal belongings left behind, a discarded shoe, a frayed piece of fabric became silent witnesses to the lives that had been brutally cut short. Each artifact became proof of a human story, a connection to the lives that had been taken within these very walls. The emotional impact deepened as I read the stories of those who had perished, their faces and names no longer just statistics, but individuals with dreams and lives unjustly stolen.

People from all walks of life were imprisoned here. Among them were renowned individuals like Dr. Gisella Perl, a gynaecologist who provided clandestine medical care to fellow prisoners, and Etty Hillesum, a writer whose diaries documented her experiences and thoughts during the Holocaust. There were artists like Dina Gottliebova, who was forced to paint portraits for the camp's infamous Dr. Josef Mengele, and intellectuals such as Viktor Frankl, a neurologist and psychiatrist who survived Auschwitz and later wrote "Man's Search for Meaning," reflecting on his experiences and the search for purpose amidst suffering. The presence of such diverse and talented individuals, all brought to the same cruel fate, highlighted the indiscriminate nature of the Holocaust's brutality. Each of these individuals brought their unique talents and perspectives to the camp, and their stories provide a deeper understanding of the diverse lives that were cruelly interrupted. The artifacts were not just remains of the past, they were parts of lives that were extinguished too soon. Scientists, artists, writers, and everyday people all shared the same tragic fate within these walls.

The human faces behind the figures became more than just numbers, they were individuals with dreams, fears, and aspirations. The personal belongings and stories of these people brought a heartfelt connection, a recognition of the lives and talents that were lost. The artifacts served as a reminder of the potential that was stolen and the importance of remembering and honouring those who perished.

Image captured by the author ©

This photograph captures historically significant moment displayed at the Auschwitz 1. The image shows a group of Jewish prisoners arriving at Auschwitz II-Birkenau in 1944, specifically highlighting the arrival of Jews from Hungary. The photo depicts men, women, and children disembarking from a train, likely after a long and arduous journey under inhumane conditions. The expressions on the faces of the newly arrived prisoners reflect a mixture of confusion, fear, and uncertainty as they face the unknown horrors of the concentration camp.

This photograph captures a wall of black-and-white images of people who were imprisoned in Auschwitz, highlighting the contrast between their innocent faces and the horrific backdrop of their reality. Each one, dressed in the camp's striped uniform, stares out from the past, their expressions, a reminder of the brutality they endured. Below these images, a display case holds small garments, some tattered and worn, representing the personal belongings that once provided a semblance of normalcy in their young lives.

Page 43

CHAPTER 4
FACES IN PHOTOGRAPHS

The journey through Auschwitz was a relentless immersion into history, but it was the faces captured in black and white photographs that truly struck deep and left an indelible impression. As I entered the exhibit hall, my eyes were immediately drawn to the wall of photographs, each face a poignant reminder of the lives lost. The air grew still, with the countless stories captured in the silent gazes of the victims. I felt a pervasive silence settle over me, as if their countless stories had momentarily frozen the time. The heavy silence in the room was palpable, broken only by the soft shuffle of footsteps and the occasional murmur of hushed voices.

Photographs on the walls were like a mosaic of faces captured in a timeless moment. These were not just images, they were windows into a past that bore witness to indescribable suffering. The impact of those photographs was immediate and instinctive, a collective gasp echoed through the room, as if the very air had been sucked out by the gravity of the images before us. Each face told a story, their lives interrupted and dreams were shattered. Their eyes which were the windows to their soul, conveyed a mix of spirit, fear, and sometimes a little hope. The photographs were not merely portraits, they were mirrors reflecting the humankind that had been extinguished within the boundaries of Auschwitz and the musty smell of old wood and faint traces of dust added to the atmosphere, making the experience even more tangible.

One photograph that particularly moved me was of a young girl, her eyes wide with a mix of innocence and fear. I couldn't help but wonder about her story. Who were her parents? What dreams did she have before being thrust into this nightmare? The sheer vulnerability in her expression was heart-wrenching. This was the face of Czesława Kwoka, a 14-year-old Polish girl, one of the many children taken to Auschwitz. Her photograph, taken shortly after her arrival, shows the bruise on her face, a result of being beaten by an SS guard during her intake at the camp. Czesława, like many others, did not survive, she was killed in the gas chambers just months after her arrival. Her photograph, a image of innocence lost, remains one of the reminders of the brutality faced by children in the camp.

As I stood before the photographs, a great sense of responsibility settled upon me. Each individual represented in those frames was more than a number, they were unique and had irreplaceable lives. Anticipating that they were individuals who had laughed, loved, and dreamed like us. Another photograph that stood out was of a couple, Mala Zimetbaum and Edek Galiński, their faces lined with the hardships they had endured even before arriving at Auschwitz. Mala, a Belgian Jew of Polish descent, and Edek, a Polish political prisoner, met and fell in love within the camp's walls. Mala was known for her bravery and compassion, often helping other prisoners by using her position as a translator and courier. The couple planned a daring escape from Auschwitz in June 1944, with Edek disguised as an SS guard and Mala as a prisoner being transferred. Unfortunately, they were caught just days later. After their capture, they were sentenced to death, but they defied the Nazis even in their final moments. As she was being led to her execution, Mala attempted to slit her wrists to avoid the agony of the gas chamber. Edek, upon hearing this, tried to escape again but was caught and hanged. Their love and courage have since become symbols of resistance in the face of unimaginable evil. The strength and resolve in their eyes spoke volumes, and I found myself deeply moved by their silent fortitude. These photographs were taken by Nazi officers as part of their meticulous documentation, a grotesque attempt to chronicle their inhumane acts. As I gazed upon the images of these young pairs, a contrast emerged between the innocence of childhood and the sinister backdrop of Auschwitz. Twins, often brought to the camp with their families, faced an unimaginable fate. Subjected to Mengele's ruthless experiments in the name of pseudoscience, their lives took a dark and twisted turn within the boundaries of Auschwitz. Josef Mengele, infamously known as the "Angel of Death," performed horrific medical experiments on twins, including injections of chemicals into their eyes to change eye colour, amputations, and other procedures without anaesthesia. Many twins died as a result of these experiments, while others were killed so their bodies could be dissected. Those who survived were left with deep psychological and physical scars. The image of a pair of twins holding hands, their bond unbroken even in the face of such terror, brought tears to my eyes. Their togetherness amidst the chaos was both heartbreaking and inspiring. The bond shared between siblings became a source of both solace and anguish as they navigated the horrors of Auschwitz together. The twins became involuntary subjects in Mengele's mad quest, their bodies and souls forever scarred by the cruelty inflicted upon them. René and Renate Guttmann, twins born in 1937 in Czechoslovakia, were just six years old when they were deported to Auschwitz with their family in 1943. Upon arrival, the twins were separated from their parents and became subjects of cruel experiments. Mengele, obsessed with studying twins, subjected René and Renate to horrific procedures, including injections and invasive tests without anesthesia. Stripped of their identity, the twins endured immense suffering, while their mother, Ita, was left devastated, not knowing the fate of her children. As the war drew to a close in 1945, Auschwitz was evacuated, and the surviving prisoners, including the twins, were forced on a death march. In the chaos, René and Renate were separated. Renate was eventually found and placed in a Catholic orphanage in Eastern Europe, while René was adopted by a family in the United States, growing up unaware of his true identity. Ita Guttmann survived the Holocaust and tirelessly searched for her children. She was reunited with Renate but could not find René. Decades passed before René discovered his origins in the 1980s, when Holocaust survivor organizations helped reconnect him with his sister. The reunion was filled with both joy and sorrow as the twins came to terms with the lost years and the trauma they had endured. The story of René and Renate Guttmann is a powerful testament to the lasting impact of the Holocaust on survivors and their families. Their reunion, after years of separation, shows how strong family bonds can be and reminds us that hope and love can survive even the hardest times.

Another twin story of Eva Mozes Kor and her twin sister Miriam highlights the resilience of the human spirit even in the face of such immense cruelty. Eva Mozes Kor and her twin sister, Miriam, were born on January 31, 1934, in the small village of Portz, Romania. As Jewish children growing up during the rise of Nazi Germany, their lives were upended in 1944 when their family was forced into a cattle car and deported to Auschwitz-Birkenau. The journey was harrowing, and upon arrival at the camp, Eva and Miriam were immediately separated from their parents and older siblings, who were sent to the gas chambers. The twins were selected for Mengele's experiments. The twins were injected with unknown substances, measured, and monitored as part of Mengele's twisted pursuit of genetic research. The experiments were brutal and often life-threatening. Eva recalled being injected with a deadly disease and told that she had only two weeks to live. Determined to survive, Eva fought against the illness and miraculously recovered. However, she was left with severe physical and emotional scars. Miriam, too, endured similar experiments, but their experiences left her with lifelong health complications. The twins survived Auschwitz, and after the camp's liberation in 1945, they were among the few survivors of Mengele's experiments. Eva and Miriam were eventually reunited with an aunt and moved to Israel, where they began to rebuild their lives. Despite the trauma they endured, the sisters remained close, supporting each other through the challenges of living with the memories of Auschwitz. In later years, Eva Mozes Kor became an outspoken advocate for Holocaust education and forgiveness. She founded the CANDLES Holocaust Museum and Education Center in Indiana, dedicated to preserving the stories of Holocaust survivors and educating future generations. Eva's journey toward forgiveness, including her decision to forgive the Nazis, sparked both admiration and controversy, but she remained committed to her belief in the healing power of forgiveness. Miriam, however, suffered from health problems caused by the experiments and passed away In 1993. Eva continued her work in Holocaust remembrance until her death in 2019. Seeing their photographs and listening to their stories , I couldn't help but marvel at their courage and the unbreakable bond that helped them survive such unimaginable horrors. The images and stories of these twins serve as a reminder of the human cost of hatred and intolerance.

In the hall, the diversity of the faces struck me, the young and old, men and women, children and adults. Looking into the eyes of those captured in the photographs, I felt a deep connection to their humanity and a sense of injustice at the horrors they endured. The nature of their selection for extermination became painfully evident.

In the silence of the exhibit hall, I felt a deep desire to connect with the human side of history. The photographs showed the concept of the Holocaust, grounding it in the reality of faces that had once had life. It became a personal excursion, a journey into the lives of those who had walked the same earth, breathed the same air, and felt the same sun on their faces.

The more I studied each photograph, the more the victims ceased to be distant historical figures, they became neighbours, friends, and family. Their faces were no longer just images, they were personal stories etched into my memory. It was an invitation to empathise, to bridge the gap and recognise the shared humanity that bound us together. The photographs were not just pictures of the past, they were bridges connecting the present to an ever-living history. Each gaze seemed to reach out, asking not to be forgotten, urging us to remember their lives and their suffering.

As I left the exhibit, the faces resided in my thoughts, like a witnesses demanding remembrance. The impact of viewing those photographs had pegged itself into my consciousness, compelling me to carry out their stories forward. The faces captured in black and white, I found a call to action, a commitment to ensure that the individual lives represented would never be forgotten, and that their stories would forever be remembered. The emotional resonance of their images lingered, a silent yet powerful reminder of the importance of memory and the enduring human spirit. The journey through Auschwitz had become a personal encounter with the human faces of history. These photographs, each telling a unique story, transformed my understanding of the Holocaust from abstract history to deeply personal reality.

This image shows used canisters of Zyklon B gas, which were used in the gas chambers at Nazi concentration camps during the Holocaust. Zyklon B was a cyanide-based pesticide that the Nazis repurposed for mass murder. The label "GIFTGAS" indicates poison gas, with the skull and crossbones serving as a warning of its lethal contents. This image underscores the horrific and systematic nature of the Holocaust.

Image captured by the author ©

This photograph captures the entrance to a significant and tragic part of Auschwitz, marked by a sign reading "DROGA ŚMIERCI" or "THE ROAD OF DEATH." The view through the doorway reveals a historic black-and-white photograph of prisoners being led to their deaths, further emphasising the gravity of this path. This corridor, known as "The Road of Death," was a passage that many prisoners were forced to walk, leading them to the gas chambers.

Chapter 5
Walking Through History

The guided tour through Auschwitz's museum took me on an emotional journey into the tragic events of history. A knowledgeable guide led the way, turning the museum into a space of remembrance. Carefully curated artifacts and exhibits unfolded a chronological narrative of horror, each step through the halls feeling like a descent into the past. One of the first exhibits that caught my attention was a large pile of shoes, each pair representing a stolen existence. Seeing those shoes, some small enough to belong to children, reminded me of the individuality and humanity of each victim. A direct confrontation with the atrocities that had left their mark on the face of the mother earth.

At the heart of the museum were historical documents and artifacts. Original letters, diaries, and official records provided an intimate look into the lives of those who had faced the horrors of Auschwitz. One particular diary, written by a young girl, stood out to me. Her entries, filled with dreams and fears, abruptly ended, leaving a heavy silence that spoke volumes about the abruptness of her fate. Artifacts, from makeshift tools crafted by prisoners to poetry scratched onto walls and doors, revealed a human spirit that refused to be extinguished. Engaging with these pieces became a way to connect not just with the events but with the individuals who had once sought solace and support. Another artifact that moved me deeply was a set of

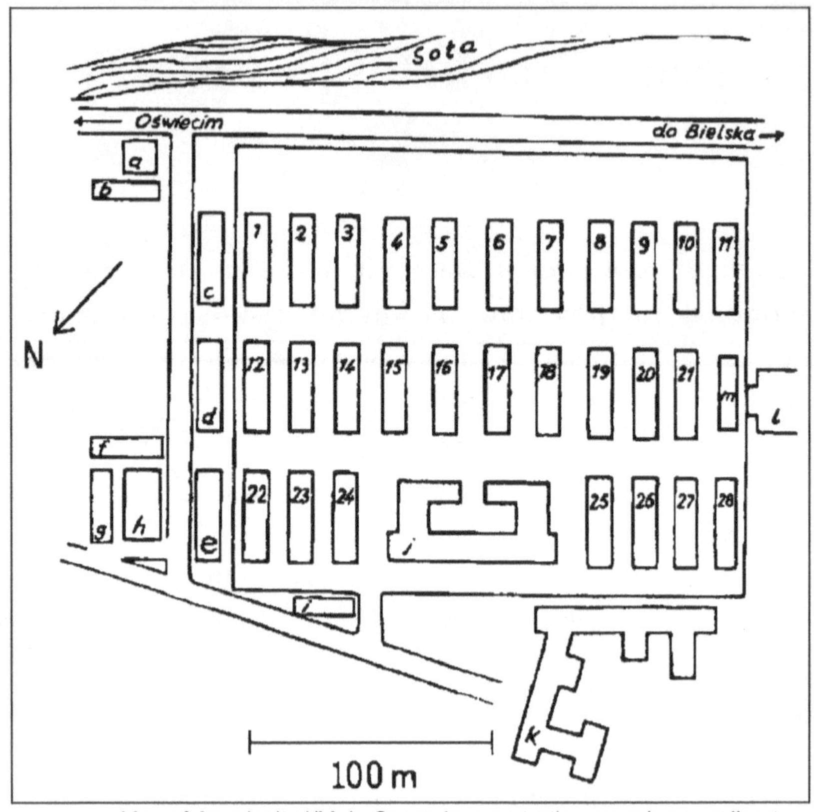

Map of Auschwitz I/Main Camp (concentration camp), according to the information brochure of the Auschwitz State Museum in 1991.

Block 1 – 28: inmate barracks

a: commandant's house
b: main guard station
c: camp commandant's office
d: administration building
e: SS hospital
f,g: political division

h: Crematorium I with "gas chamber"
i: guard station near camp entrance gate (block leader room)
j: camp kitchen
k: inmate registration building
l: camp warehouse, theatre building
m: new laundry

Auschwitz 1 Camp Layout : Information brochure of the Auschwitz State Museum, 1991.

eyeglasses, twisted and broken. They symbolised the clarity that was stolen from their owner, both literally and metaphorically, as they were thrust into the nightmare of Auschwitz.

As you step into the solemn expanse of Auschwitz, each block unveils a chilling chapter of history, bearing witness to the unimaginable atrocities committed here. Block 10 stands as a testament to the inhumane medical experiments conducted. Here, innocent lives were subjected to torturous trials, leaving scars that extend far beyond the physical. Many prisoners became unwilling subjects for medical experiments, with Dr. Josef Mengele, leading much of this gruesome research, particularly focusing on twins and dwarfs. One of the most notorious experiments I learned was injecting dye into inmates' eyes to observe any colour changes. The experiments extended to forced sterilisation, the use of harmful substances, starvation, electroshocks, and uterine injections, constituting barbaric acts of cruelty. Seeing the instruments used for these experiments, displayed with clinical coldness, shocked me. It was hard to believe the cruelty and indifference needed to perform such acts. These experiments unfolded within Block 10, also referred to as the *"Krankenbau" or Hospital Barrack,* located inside Auschwitz. The conditions were deplorable, leading to the death of many and severe health problems for those who survived these horrific procedures.

Venturing into Block 11 sends shivers down the core. Known as the Death Block, it housed torture cells and execution sites, embodying the ruthless brutality of the Nazi regime. The air here seems to carry cries of the anguish endured by those who faced the cruelest of fates. One cell in particular, known as the starvation cell, left a lasting impact on me. Standing in front of it, I could almost hear the silent screams of those who had perished within its walls. Prisoners in Auschwitz faced brutal treatment from guards and kapos for even the smallest rule violations. Originally called block 13, block 11 of Auschwitz I became a prison within the prison for suspected resistance inmates. Inside this barrack, the Cell 22 was a dark standing cell split into four sections and each section measured less than 1 meter square, housing four prisoners in cramped conditions. Air came through a small vent, offering little relief from the oppressive environment. Prisoners might spend several nights in Cell 22 in that closed space, often emerging barely able to stand, their spirits crushed under the relentless weight of suffering. The atmosphere in Block 11 was suffocating, as the reality of the pain and suffering endured here became overwhelmingly palpable. It was a place where hope was systematically extinguished, replaced by the overwhelming presence of death and despair.

Adjacent to Block 11 stands the Wall, where countless prisoners faced the cold finality of execution. It is called the *"Death Wall,"* which served as an execution site, particularly for Poles sentenced to death by a criminal court in the General Government area. The first executions, occurring on November 11, 1941, Poland's National Independence Day, involved shooting inmates in the back of the head. Stripped and hands tied, 151 accused were led to the wall one by one. Approximately 4,500 Polish political prisoners, including resistance members, faced execution at this wall. An additional 10,000 unregistered Poles were brought in for execution, with an estimated 1,000 Soviet prisoners of war meeting the same fate. The absolute silence surrounding this wall is a reminder of the lives lost to senseless brutality. Standing before the Death Wall, I felt an overwhelming sense of sorrow and anger. The cold stones seemed to pulse with the memory of the countless lives ended here.

Another hidden secret lies within Block 24, which served a different, more sinister purpose, it was the camp's brothel. Established in 1943 as part of an SS scheme to incentivise prisoners to work harder, the brothel was a place of unimaginable suffering. Women, often selected from the Ravensbrück concentration camp, were forced into sexual slavery, enduring brutal conditions and frequent abuse. Their lives were a living hell, as they were forced to serve prisoners and guards alike, with little hope of survival. This aspect of the camp's operation is rarely discussed, yet it reflects the depths of human degradation that occurred within Auschwitz's walls.

Block 21 served as one of the camp's surgical wards, but its function went beyond legitimate medical care. Here, surgeries were performed, often without proper anesthesia, on prisoners who had little hope of survival. While some legitimate procedures were conducted, many surgeries served as a front for covert euthanasia programs. Prisoners deemed too weak or unfit were often given lethal injections, disguised as treatments. The medical records from this block were meticulously kept, yet they hide the reality of unnecessary and often fatal surgeries performed on prisoners. This block, under the guise of care, became a place where life and death were manipulated by the whims of Nazi doctors.

Block 20, known as the "Prisoner's Hospital," was where prisoners with contagious diseases were housed. This block was designated for those suffering from illnesses such as tuberculosis, erysipelas, and severe diarrhea. While ostensibly a place of care, the conditions were horrific, with overcrowding, lack of medical supplies, and minimal attention leading to a high mortality rate. The block was often isolated to prevent the spread of disease, and those who were brought here rarely survived. It was a place of immense suffering, where the sick were left to die in deplorable conditions, their deaths often recorded with little accuracy or care.

Moving further, the gas chambers and crematoriums emerge as harrowing symbols of mass extermination. In the beginning of September 1941, the first use of gas chambers for mass killings happened at Auschwitz. Approximately 850 prisoners, including Soviet prisoners of war and unwell Polish inmates, lost their lives to 'Zyklon B' in the basement of block 11 in Auschwitz I. In order to keep the victims calm, they were falsely informed that they were undergoing a process of disinfection and de-lousing. The unsuspecting prisoners would undress before being led into the gas chamber, where they faced a tragic fate. Seeing the remnants of these gas chambers was an indescribable experience. The walls, now silent, bore witness to the final moments of thousands of innocent lives. The sheer scale of human suffering that unfolded within these walls is beyond comprehension. The gas used, Zyklon B, left an indelible mark on the annals of human history.

In the grim landscape of Nazi death camps during the Holocaust, a group known as the Sonderkommandos emerged. The term, originating from German and translating to "Special Unit," encapsulated a harrowing reality for those forced into its ranks. Composed predominantly of prisoners, often of Jewish descent, the Sonderkommandos faced an unimaginable choice. Assist in the disposal of gas chamber victims or meet their own demise. The gravity of this decision loomed large over their lives, tethering their survival to the unspeakable task at hand. Reading about the Sonderkommandos, I felt a deep sense of empathy for these individuals. Their forced complicity in the horrors around them was a tragic testament to the depths of human suffering. The duties assigned to the Sonderkommandos went beyond the mere mechanics of death camp operations. They were tasked with guiding victims into the gas chambers and, perhaps even more chillingly, handling the aftermath. Stripped of their humanity, they became custodians of the deceased, extracting personal effects such as jewellery, hair, and gold from teeth before ushering the bodies towards cremation. The life of a Sonderkommando was one of perpetual horror. Isolated from the general prison population due to their status as witnesses to mass murder, they lived with the constant awareness that their own existence hung by the thinnest of threads. Will there be an existence after this? Their life expectancy was tragically short, as they were systematically killed and replaced, their roles demanding a psychological toll that few could endure. Many Sonderkommandos, battling their duties, chose to end their own lives. Their lives was a dark existence, caught between the horror of their tasks and the inescapable reality that survival in such circumstances came at a dire moral cost. Despite the overwhelming despair, some Sonderkommandos took incredible risks to document what they witnessed, secretly burying photographs and written testimonies in the grounds around the crematoriums, hoping that these records would one day bear witness to the truth. The story of the Sonderkommandos stands as a reminder of the dehumanising depths to which the Holocaust descended. Their forced complicity in the machinery of death reflects the twisted logic of an era where cruelty knew no bounds. The Sonderkommandos, witnesses to tragedy, speak to the moral complexities faced by those ensnared in the most devastating phase of human history.

The scratches on the walls of the gas chambers, left by desperate hands, bore silent witness to the final struggle of the victims. Each mark felt like a cry for help, echoing through the ages. These marks, etched by those facing imminent death, berar witness to the struggle for survival amid the encroaching darkness. As you walk through history in Auschwitz, I absorbed these chilling details and facts. The gas chambers, crematoriums, and solemn blocks carry the collective memory of unspeakable horrors. This journey demands reflection on the strength of the human spirit in the face of extreme darkness, ensuring that the voices silenced within these walls are never forgotten.

Interacting with the exhibits meant grappling with the harsh reality of genocide. One particularly harrowing exhibit was a display of human hair, taken from the victims and used for various purposes by the Nazis. The sheer volume of hair, collected and displayed, was a reminder of the industrial scale of the atrocities committed. Rooms filled with confiscated possessions like a mountain of shoes, stacks of suitcases, and heaps of discarded clothing, resonated with an absolute silence. Each item served as a reminder of lives abruptly taken, bearing witness to the brutality pervasive in every corner of the camp.

As I exited, a deep feeling enveloped me. The guided tour through the exhibits had enhanced a mere chronological walkthrough. It had been an emotional rollercoaster, each artifact and exhibit pulling me deeper into the tragic reality of Auschwitz. It had been an invitation to bear witness to the darkest moments of history. Leaving the museum, I felt a renewed sense of duty to carry these memories forward, ensuring that the stories of Auschwitz are never forgotten.

Image captured by the author ©

The photograph of the utensils conveys a narrative of daily life amidst the unimaginable horrors of the concentration camp. In the simplicity of the photo, rows upon rows of utensils. Pots, pans, and cutlery, bear witness to the ordinary routines that persisted in the middle of the extraordinary cruelty of the Holocaust. Each utensil carries the stories of countless meals shared in communal kitchens, the whispered conversations, and the quiet acts of solidarity that sustained prisoners through the darkest of times. Through the lens of remembrance, the photograph offers a glimpse into the resilience of the human spirit.

Image captured by the author ©

The photograph captures a tableau of loss and despair. The silent testimony of lives abruptly shattered by the relentless machinery of genocide. Rows upon rows of abandoned luggage, piled high and stretching into the distance, bear witness to the unimaginable horrors. Each suitcase, once filled with cherished possessions and dreams of a brighter future, now stands as a reminder of the human cost of hatred and intolerance. The faded initials, the worn leather handles, speak volumes of the individuals who once carried them, their identities erased, their stories lost to the winds of history. In the calmness of the photograph, there is a sense of absence, a void left by those who left them behind, a void that can never be filled.

The photograph of the reading glasses at Auschwitz offers a glimpse into the lives that once occupied the desolate landscape of the camp. Rows upon rows of spectacles, each pair bearing the imprint of its owner, serve as a silent testament. These glasses, once cherished symbols of intellect and vision, now stand as sorrow-laden relics of lives ended by the brutality of genocide. In their frames lies the reflection of countless stories. Stories of survivals, of courage, of unfulfilled dreams. Each pair of glasses bears witness to the untold suffering.

This photograph serves as a reminder of the deep impact of the Holocaust on individuals' lives. Each prosthetic limb and walking aid represents the physical and emotional scars borne by those who endured the horrors of Auschwitz. Through this image, we honour the courage of the survivors while also acknowledging the immense loss suffered by countless others. It is a solemn tribute to the enduring legacy of suffering and survival in the face of unimaginable adversity.

Image captured by the author ©

This photograph captures the "Wall of Death" at Auschwitz I, a site where many executions were carried out during the Holocaust. The wall, constructed from dark stone and backed by red brick, is an evocative and chilling reminder of the brutal realities of the concentration camp. Prisoners, particularly those who attempted escape or were involved in resistance activities, were often executed by firing squad in front of this wall. The wall has a textured appearance, with visible wear and bullet marks, evidencing the numerous lives that ended here. The Wall of Death is a crucial part of the museum's narrative, emphasising the importance of remembering the atrocities committed to prevent such horrors from occurring again.

Image captured by the author ©

The photo depicts a tall, wooden guard tower set against an overcast sky inside Auschwitz II-Birkenau, evoking a sense of solemnity. Guard towers like this one were used by Nazi SS guards to surveil the prisoners and ensure no one could escape the camp's confines. These towers were strategically placed around the perimeter to provide a clear view of the entire camp, allowing guards to monitor and control the movements of prisoners at all times.

CHAPTER 6
BIRKENAU'S VASTNESS

The trip to Auschwitz reached a significant moment as I arrived at Auschwitz II-Birkenau, 3 kilometres from Auschwitz I. The scene unfolded in front of me, a vast display of emptiness and memory. Standing at the entrance, the sheer size of the site left me breathless. The quietness seemed to stretch endlessly, creating an almost surreal atmosphere. An expansive area that appeared to stretch forever, bearing witness to the immense suffering of humanity. Covering over 400 acres, Birkenau consisted of several sections, including the main camp area and the extermination facilities. The sheer scale of suffering and death that occurred here, stands as a testament to the horrors of the Holocaust.

Upon arrival, men, women, and children were forcibly separated. Families were torn apart, often never to see each other again. The women's camp, located in the northeastern part of Birkenau, housed female prisoners from various backgrounds, including Jews, Roma, political dissidents, and others deemed enemies of the Nazi regime. Conditions in the women's camp were harsh and inhuman, with overcrowded barracks, inadequate sanitation facilities, and rationed food. Women were subjected to forced labor, medical experiments, and the constant threat of violence from guards. The men's camp, similarly brutal, forced male prisoners into gruelling labor, suffering under the constant threat of beatings, starvation, and execution. Children, if not sent directly to the gas chambers, faced the same brutal conditions or were subjected to horrific medical experiments, particularly those conducted by Dr. Josef Mengele.

The separation and the distinct sections of the camp underscored the systematic and calculated nature of the Nazi regime's cruelty, each area within Birkenau contributing to the comprehensive machinery of genocide. The men's camp occupied the southwestern portion of Birkenau. Like the women's camp, the men's section consisted of rows of barracks surrounded by electrified fences and guard towers. Male prisoners were forced to perform gruelling labor tasks, often under inhumane conditions, and were subjected to arbitrary punishment and abuse by SS guards. The abuse included physical beatings that left many prisoners severely injured or even dead. Starvation was a common method of control, with prisoners receiving inadequate rations insufficient for survival. Psychological torture was also rampant, with guards employing tactics designed to break the prisoner's spirits, such as forced standing for hours, public humiliation, and the constant threat of execution. This relentless mistreatment aimed to destroy the prisoners, both physically and mentally, stripping away any semblance of hope and dignity.

Despite being segregated by gender, both the men's and women's camps at Birkenau shared the same overarching purpose to facilitate the systematic extermination of those deemed undesirable by the Nazi regime. The camp infrastructure, including the gas chambers and crematoria, operated indiscriminately, claiming the lives of countless men and women. Throughout Birkenau, the horrors of the Holocaust were substantial, with the pervasive presence of suffering, death, and despair. The separation of men and women within the camp complex did not diminish the collective trauma experienced by all who were imprisoned there. Instead, it served as a reminder of the systematic brutality and inhumanity of the Nazi regime's genocidal policies.

Moving from Auschwitz I to Birkenau held special meaning. As the landscape widened, so did the historical weight. The vast expanse of Birkenau, with its rows upon rows of barracks and the silence that enveloped the area, was overwhelming. Birkenau wasn't just another part of the camp, it embodied the organised and industrialised nature of the Holocaust. The train tracks, extending into the distance, served as a reminder of the countless arrivals that had once resonated with the screech of metal wheels and the anxious whispers of fear. Walking along these tracks, I could almost hear the whispers of those who had arrived, filled with a mix of hope and dread.

The vastness of Birkenau unfolded like a quiet tribute, a memorial to the multitudes whose footsteps had once resounded through its barren expanses. The remnants of watchtowers and electrified fences marked the horizon, each element bearing witness to the inhumane mechanisms that had operated within this space.

Walking through Birkenau felt like navigating a graveyard of memories. A cemetery without headstones, where the sky itself seemed to be the sole witness to the atrocities committed. The ruins of barracks, barely visible amidst the vastness, hinted at the barbarism that had occurred under the guise of order and efficiency. Coming to terms with the horrors of Birkenau was an exercise in witnessing the unimaginable. The sheer scale of the site surpassed the limits of comprehension, challenging my ability to grasp the magnitude of suffering that had unfolded

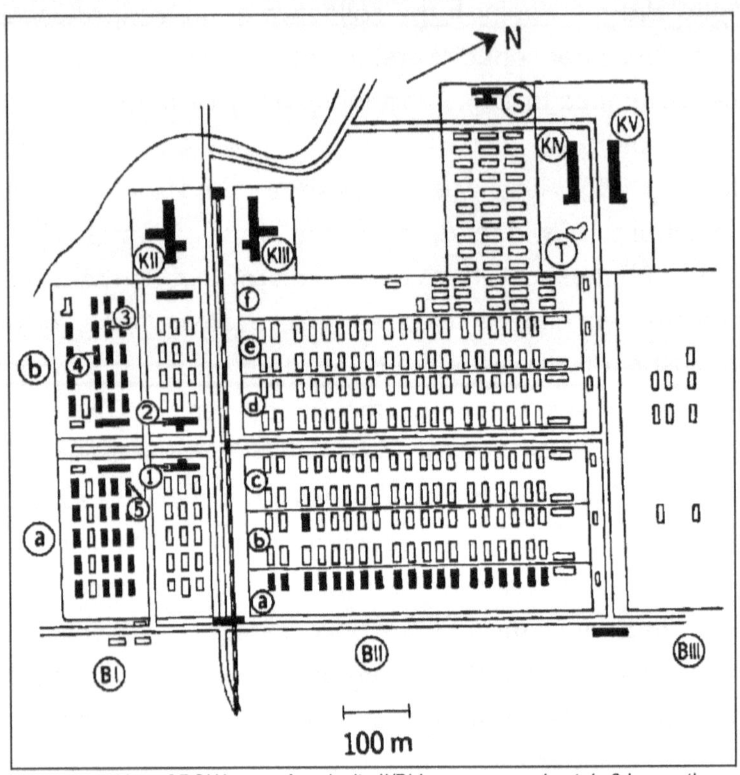

Map of POW camp Auschwitz II/Birkenau, approximately 2 km north-west of the main camp, construction situation as of the end of 1944. The shaded buildings still exist, some of them, however, only in the form of ruins or foundations (Crematoria II-V), the rest having been torn down by Polish civilians for building materials after the war. According to the information brochure of the Auschwitz State Museum, 1991.

BI-III: building sector I to III
BIa/b: women's camp
BIIa: quarantine camp
BIIb: family camp
BIIc: Hungarian camp
BIId: men's camp
BIIe: gypsy camp
BIIf: inmate hospital
K II: Crematorium II with "gas chamber"
K III: Crematorium III with "gas chamber"
K IV: Crematorium IV with "gas chamber"
K V: Crematorium V with "gas chamber"
S: "Zentralsauna," hot-air/steam disinfestation
T: pond
1: building sector 5a – Zyklon B disinfestation
2: building sector 5b – Zyklon B disinfestation
3: inmate barracks no. 13
4: inmate barracks no. 20
5: inmate barracks no. 3

Auschwitz II-Birkenau Camp Layout: Information brochure of the Auschwitz State Museum, 1991.

within its boundaries. Each step felt like a journey through a rift of historical horror as if some oppressive force of the past pressed down heavily, casting a shadow over the present.

Amidst the ruins and remnants, the question arises, What was the purpose of constructing such a vast and sprawling camp? The answer, though harrowing, became clear. Birkenau was designed not just as a concentration camp but as an extermination centre, a factory of death where the machinery of genocide operated with cold efficiency. The sheer scale of Birkenau was intended to maximise the Nazis' ability to carry out mass murder with ruthless efficiency. Contemplating the purpose of the camp's construction meant facing the grim reality that every element of Birkenau had been meticulously planned to facilitate mass murder. The crematoria and gas chambers, disguised as showers, stood as macabre testaments to the calculated cruelty that defined the Holocaust. Standing before these structures, I was struck by the cold, clinical approach taken to orchestrate such vast human suffering.

The air was thick with the stench of decay, a contrast to the grey sky above. The smell of death and suffering permeated every inch of the camp, clinging to every breath I took. As I walked through, the smell only grew stronger, a sickening reminder of the atrocities that took place here. As I wandered through the desolate expanses, the chilly wind carried cries of the past. The purpose of Birkenau's construction crystallised as a symbol of the darkest corners of human capability. The silence was broken only by the whispers of the wind, carrying with it the memories of those who had suffered and perished here.

A manifestation of ideological madness, and a chilling reminder of the consequences when humanity surrenders to the forces of hatred and prejudice. The enormity of Birkenau demanded contemplation, not just of the historical events that transpired, but of the collective responsibility to ensure that such horrors never repeated. The journey through Birkenau became a silent pledge, an acknowledgment of the past, a commitment to remembrance, and a solemn vow to safeguard the future from the shadows that lingered within the vastness of that landscape. As I moved towards Crematoria, the vastness and silence of the camp remained with me, a powerful reminder of the importance of memory and the need to ensure that such atrocities are never repeated.

Image captured by the author ©

Upon entering Auschwitz II-Birkenau, through the infamous main gate, this building, located on the right side, is one of the men's brick barracks. The building is surrounded by barbed wire fences, symbolising the severe entrapment and isolation experienced by those held within. This building, like many others in Auschwitz II-Birkenau, served as a barrack where countless male prisoners endured unimaginable suffering.

Image captured by the author ©

This wooden freight car, used by the Nazis during the Holocaust, transported millions of people to extermination camps like Auschwitz-Birkenau. Crowded with up to 100 people, these cars had no ventilation, food, or sanitation. Many died during the brutal journey. Upon arrival, survivors faced immediate selection for labor or death, marking a key element in the Nazis' genocidal Final Solution.

Image captured by the author ©

This photograph captures the remnants of a gas chamber at Auschwitz II-Birkenau, a chilling testament to the horrors of the Holocaust. The collapsed structure, surrounded by rubble, stands under a foreboding sky, its broken walls and twisted metal highlighting the brutality that occurred within.

CHAPTER 7
THE REMAINS OF CREMATORIA

As I walked through the camp, I was taken aback by the physical remains of gas chambers and crematoria structures that stood as silent witnesses to the organised machinery of mass extermination. While standing before these physical remains of human cruelty, I was overwhelmed with a deep anguish and disbelief. These structures, though largely destroyed by the Nazis as they attempted to hide the evidence of their crimes, still bear significance in the collective memory of humanity. The crematoria were composed of three main sections: a dressing room, a gas chamber, and a furnace room. In crematoria II and III, the dressing room and gas chamber were located underground, while in IV and V, they were situated on the ground floor.

The SS officers misled victims by informing them that they needed to take a shower and undergo cleansing procedures. Victims would undress in the dressing room before entering the gas chamber, which bore signs indicating Bath/Disinfection rooms. These remains appeared like ghostly guardians, their decayed walls and twisted metal serving as reminders of a past too horrifying to fully grasp. The gas chambers, disguised as innocent shower rooms, testified to the deceitfulness of the Nazi regime. Above, the chimneys of the crematoria loomed, symbols of the efficiency with which human lives were turned to ashes. The gas chambers and crematoria at Birkenau were constructed as part of the camp's expansion to facilitate mass murder on an industrial scale. They were built between 1942 and 1943 as the Nazi regime intensified its efforts to exterminate the prisoners. The gas chambers and crematoria were located in close proximity to the railway lines that brought deportees to Birkenau. This location facilitated the efficient and rapid processing of victims upon their arrival at the camp.

In their shadow, I felt a deep connection to the countless souls who met their end within these walls. These remains were more than just architectural structures, they were gateways into the darkest depths of human history. The very bricks and mortar seemed to resonate with the cries of those who had perished. A symphony of despair that eclipsed the ages. The expert guide's explanation of the gas chambers and crematoria mechanics provided a chilling insight into the industrialised scale of genocide. The cold efficiency with which the Nazis implemented mass extermination left me grappling with a horror that went beyond anything I had read in history books. Before the development and implementation of gas chambers in extermination camps, the Nazis experimented with various methods to execute Jews and other prisoners. Initially, mass shootings were employed by the Einsatzgruppen, mobile killing units that followed the German army into Eastern Europe. These units would round up victims, force them to dig their own graves, and then execute them by firing squad. However, this method proved to be psychologically taxing on the soldiers and logistically inefficient. In search of a more efficient means of mass murder, the Nazis turned to gas. One of the first experiments with gas took place at the Brandenburg Euthanasia Center in Germany. Here, carbon monoxide was used to kill disabled and mentally ill patients as part of the T4 Euthanasia

Program, which aimed to eliminate those deemed "unworthy of life." Victims were led into gas chambers disguised as shower rooms, and carbon monoxide gas was pumped in, resulting in their deaths within minutes.

The gas chambers, where unsuspecting victims were led under false promises, became chambers of death, where Zyklon B gas extinguished life with terrifying efficiency. Originally developed as a pesticide in the early 1920s, it was a cyanide-based compound created by Fritz Haber, a Nobel Prize-winning chemist, and later produced by the German company Degesch. Zyklon B consisted of hydrogen cyanide (prussic acid), a stabilizer, and a warning odorant. Initially used to fumigate ships, buildings, and warehouses, its application took a sinister turn when the Nazis discovered its lethal potential for mass murder. The use of Zyklon B in the gas chambers represented a horrifying blend of scientific progress and moral decay, where technology meant to protect life was repurposed to end it on an industrial scale. The transformation of a pesticide into a weapon of genocide is the irony of the Holocaust.The production and supply of Zyklon B to the Auschwitz camps were tightly controlled and involved multiple companies. It was primarily manufactured by two companies, Degesch and Tesch & Stabenow, with the product being distributed across the network of concentration and extermination camps. Auschwitz III, also known as Monowitz, was closely linked to the industrial complex of IG Farben, a conglomerate that produced synthetic rubber and other chemicals essential to the Nazi war effort. While Monowitz was primarily a labor camp for the production of synthetic materials, the broader industrial network of which it was a part also facilitated the distribution of chemicals, including Zyklon B. This connection between industrial production and the

Holocaust's machinery of death shows how ordinary industry was co-opted into the service of mass murder.

The gas chambers and crematoria are broken and partially destroyed because the Nazis themselves attempted to obliterate these structures to hide the evidence of their crimes as the Allied forces advanced. In late 1944 and early 1945, as Soviet troops were approaching, the Nazis dismantled and blew up the crematoria and gas chambers at Auschwitz-Birkenau in a frantic effort to erase what they had perpetrated. The destruction of these structures mirrored other desperate Nazi efforts to cover up their activities. In other parts of Europe, the Nazis also sought to destroy evidence of mass killings. For instance, Operation 1005 was initiated to exhume and burn bodies from mass graves, especially those from the Einsatzgruppen executions. Similarly, in camps like Treblinka, Sobibor, and Belzec, the Nazis dismantled and disguised extermination sites as farms or fields.

Meanwhile, the Allied forces faced a significant moral and strategic dilemma. As reports of mass exterminations at Auschwitz and other camps reached the Allies, discussions emerged about whether to bomb the camps to halt the genocide. Some argued that bombing the gas chambers and railways leading to the camps could disrupt the Nazi killing operations and potentially save lives. However, others were concerned about the high risk of killing the very prisoners they sought to save, as these camps were densely populated with innocent people. The precision bombing needed to target specific structures without causing massive collateral damage was beyond the technological capabilities of the time, adding to the complexity of the decision. Additionally, the primary focus of the Allied forces was on winning the war as swiftly as possible, believing that defeating Nazi Germany would end the atrocities.

The decision not to bomb the camps was also influenced by a lack of complete and detailed information about the scale of the atrocities being committed. Reports of the Holocaust were often fragmented and initially met with skepticism, which further complicated the decision-making process. Furthermore, logistical challenges, including the diversion of resources from other critical military operations, made it difficult to justify such an action from a strategic standpoint. The consequences of not bombing remain a topic of debate, highlighting the difficult decisions faced by the Allies in responding to the Holocaust. This decision, though controversial, was influenced by the complex realities of war, where moral choices were deeply intertwined with military strategy. The moral implications of this decision continue to resonate, as it underscores the agonising choices that must be made in the fog of war, where the lines between right and wrong are often blurred by the realities of conflict. Ultimately, the Allies chose not to bomb Auschwitz or other camps, deciding that ground troops would be the most effective means of liberation. This decision left the responsibility of stopping the atrocities to the advancing Soviet and Allied ground forces, who eventually liberated the camps and exposed the full extent of the horrors within.

In the camp, the crematoria, fueled by the remains of the deceased, revealed the horrific process of exterminating humans. The systematic nature of it all left me emotional, a realisation that genocide had been organised to a degree that defied moral comprehension. Understanding the harsh reality of genocide meant not only facing the physical remains but also grappling with the psychological and moral aftermath. The scale of destruction and the systematic cruelty cast a long shadow over the remnants. These were not just ruins, they were silent witnesses to the annihilation of innocence. Standing amidst the ruins of the crematoria, I reflected on the significance of these structures. They were more than just evidence of atrocity, they were a testament to the depths of human cruelty and the need for eternal vigilance against such evil. The gravity of the atrocities committed within these walls forced me to accept uncomfortable truths about human nature, our capacity for cruelty, susceptibility to manipulation, and the collective inaction that allowed such horrors to unfold. It was an unforgettable experience of history and a reflection on complicity through time.

Leaving the remains of the crematoria behind, the memories of the experience settled deep within me. The journey through Auschwitz reached a peak of anguish, a direct confrontation with the brutal reality of genocide that overwhelmed mere intellectual understanding. The remnants of gas chambers and crematoria stood not only as physical artifacts but as reminders of our collective responsibility to ensure that such atrocities never stain the pages of history again. This wasn't just a struggle with the past, it was a call to action to protect the future from the horrors of Auschwitz.

The building in the photo is one of the crematoriums at the Auschwitz II-Birkenau. It was damaged during the final months of World War II. As the Soviet army advanced towards Auschwitz in January 1945, the Nazis attempted to destroy evidence of their atrocities. They demolished many structures, including gas chambers and crematoriums, to hide the extent of the genocide they had perpetrated.

This photograph captures the remnants of a crematorium and gas chamber complex at Auschwitz II-Birkenau. The structure is now reduced to ruins. The site is preserved as part of the Auschwitz-Birkenau State Museum, which educates visitors about the Holocaust and serves as a memorial to the victims.

Image captured by the author ©

The photograph shows the ruins of Crematorium III at Auschwitz-Birkenau II, one of the main extermination facilities in the camp. Crematorium III, like its twin Crematorium II, was used extensively during the Holocaust for mass murder, with a gas chamber and crematorium within the structure.

This photograph captures the interior of one of the crematoria at Auschwitz 1. The image shows the industrial ovens used by the Nazis to dispose of the bodies of countless victims, a grim testament to the systematic nature of the genocide. In the foreground, the metal trolleys and rails used to transport bodies into the ovens are prominently visible, emphasising the brutal, assembly-line method of disposal.

This photograph captures the interior of a gas chamber at Auschwitz 1. The barren, concrete walls, marred with patches of peeling paint and discolouration, evoke a chilling sense of the atrocities that took place within this confined space. The simplicity and rawness of the room starkly contrast with the horrors it witnessed, making it a powerful symbol of the systematic brutality of the Holocaust. It was within these walls that countless innocent lives were extinguished, their final moments marked by unimaginable fear and suffering.

Image captured by Jean Carlo Emer, Published on November 26, 2019

Rising prominently in the background is a tall, rectangular brick chimney, part of the crematoria complex of Auschwitz 1. The chimney, with its weathered bricks, seems to pierce the overcast sky, serving as a testament to the industrial-scale extermination that took place here. The bare trees and fallen leaves enhancing the sense of desolation and remembrance. This image captures the chilling reality of Auschwitz, where nature and history converge to tell a story of immense suffering and loss, urging viewers to reflect on the past and the enduring importance of remembrance.

Image captured by the author ©

This photograph captures a view of the interior of a crematorium at Auschwitz 1. The room, with its dark and charred walls, filled with silence, echoing the unspeakable horrors that occurred within them. The central focus is the metal trolley and tracks, part of the gruesome apparatus used to transport bodies into the ovens for cremation. The beams and structure above, blackened from smoke, add to the chilling sense of the systematic brutality that defined this space.

This photograph captures the railway tracks leading into Auschwitz II-Birkenau, a powerful symbol of the mass deportations that brought millions of innocent people to their tragic fate. The tracks, stretching endlessly under a foreboding sky, evoke a sense of desolation and inevitable doom. These rails were the final journey for many, guiding trains loaded with men, women, and children to the infamous selection ramp where life and death decisions were made upon arrival.

CHAPTER 8
STORIES OF SURVIVAL AND RESISTANCE

As I ventured through the mournful expanses of Auschwitz II-Birkenau, a chapter unfolded that went beyond the shadows of despair. This chapter wasn't solely about tragedy, it sparkled with the strong spirit of human resilience and resistance. It was a journey into survival, a testament to the courage of those who defied the horrors of Birkenau and emerged as beacons of hope within its grim confines. For survivors, the memories of Auschwitz are often accompanied by intense feelings of trauma, grief, and survivor's guilt. The constant threat of death, the loss of loved ones, and the daily struggle for survival create a psychological landscape marked by despair and existential dread. Many survivors grapple with nightmares, flashbacks, and feelings of isolation long after their liberation, as documented by studies on post-traumatic stress disorder. The psychological trauma of Auschwitz extends beyond individual survivors to entire communities and generations. The legacy of trauma is passed down through families, shaping their identities and influencing their relationships with the world around them. The intergenerational transmission of trauma serves as a reminder of the enduring impact of genocide and the importance of bearing witness to the horrors of history.

At the same time, the resilience and strength of survivors offer a glimmer of hope amidst the darkness. Despite facing unimaginable suffering, many survivors have found ways to rebuild their lives and find meaning in the face of adversity. Their stories serve as a testament to the human spirit's capacity for endurance, courage, and compassion in the face of unspeakable evil. In understanding the psychological legacy of Auschwitz, we uncover grievous truths about human nature and the depths of human cruelty. It challenges us to face the darkness within ourselves and to strive for a world where such atrocities can never happen again.

The stories of survival within Auschwitz II-Birkenau were both fragile and powerful, standing firm against the unimaginable atrocities. Each tale revealed a human capacity to endure, resist, and find strength even in the face of systematic brutality. These stories emerged delicately, like petals among the thorns of history, shedding light on the unwavering determination of individuals who refused to be extinguished.

The White Rose Group: During the oppressive atmosphere of Nazi Germany, a clandestine resistance group known as the White Rose emerged as a beacon of courage and moral clarity. Comprising primarily college students from the University of Munich, including siblings Hans and Sophie Scholl, Christoph Probst, Alexander Schmorell, Willi Graf, and their philosophy professor Kurt Huber, the group undertook the dangerous mission of opposing the Nazi regime through non-violent resistance.

The White Rose was motivated by a strong belief in justice and a deep commitment to Christian ethics and human rights. They were horrified by the atrocities committed by the Nazis, including the persecution and murder of Jews and other minority groups. Their acts of defiance began in the summer of 1942, when they started producing and distributing anti-Nazi leaflets. These leaflets, written with passion and clarity, called for passive resistance against the Nazi regime and urged their fellow Germans to rise against the tyranny.

The leaflets were distributed throughout Munich and other cities, left in mailboxes, dropped in public places, and even mailed anonymously to individuals. Each leaflet ended with the phrase "Freedom!" and appealed to the moral conscience of the German people. The group's activities were not only an intellectual rebellion but also a direct challenge to the Nazi propaganda machine. They risked severe consequences, including imprisonment and death, to spread their message of resistance and hope.

One of the most significant actions taken by the White Rose occurred in February 1943. Hans and Sophie Scholl were caught distributing leaflets at the University of Munich. Sophie, in a daring act of defiance, threw a stack of leaflets from a balcony into the university's atrium, ensuring that they scattered like seeds of dissent. The Gestapo, the official secret police of Nazi Germany and in German-occupied Europe quickly arrested them, and after a brief trial, they were sentenced to death. On February 22, 1943, Hans and Sophie Scholl, along with Christoph Probst, were executed by guillotine.

The executions were intended to silence the White Rose, but instead, they amplified their message. The leaflets continued to circulate, smuggled out of Germany and reprinted by the Allies. The bravery and moral conviction of the White Rose members resonated far beyond their immediate circle, inspiring others to resist and keeping the spirit of defiance alive.

The story of the White Rose Group is prominently featured in several Holocaust museums, including the United States Holocaust Memorial Museum and the Jewish Museum in Berlin, where their bravery is honoured and their leaflets preserved. These exhibits provide a detailed account of their activities, personal letters, photographs, and the actual leaflets they distributed. The legacy of the White Rose endures as a powerful reminder of the impact that a small group of determined individuals can have in the face of overwhelming evil.

The Sonderkommando Rebellion: The Sonderkommando, Jewish prisoners who were forced to work in the crematoria, were confronted with the most horrific tasks within Auschwitz. These prisoners, aware of the atrocities being committed, harboured a deep-seated desire for resistance. In October 1944, they planned and executed a revolt, despite knowing that their chances of survival were slim.

The rebellion was meticulously planned over several months. The Sonderkommando secretly stockpiled weapons and explosives smuggled into the camp. Women prisoners who worked in munitions factories within the camp played a crucial role, passing along small amounts of gunpowder to the Sonderkommando. Among these brave women were Ala Gertner, Roza Robota, Regina Safirsztain, and Estera Wajsblum, who risked their lives to support the uprising.

On October 7, 1944, the rebellion was set into motion. The Sonderkommando at Crematorium IV, led by prisoners such as Zalmen Gradowski and Józef Deresiński, attacked the SS guards with hammers, axes, and makeshift grenades. They managed to kill several SS guards and set Crematorium IV ablaze, causing significant damage. The flames and explosions could be seen across the camp, signalling the start of the uprising.

Simultaneously, the Sonderkommando in other crematoria also rose in revolt, although with less success. The prisoners at Crematorium II attempted to join the uprising but were quickly overwhelmed by the SS guards. Despite their determination, the rebellion was swiftly and brutally suppressed by the SS, who crushed the revolt. Hundreds of Sonderkommando were killed in the fighting, and many more were executed in the aftermath.

Although the rebellion did not achieve its ultimate goal of dismantling the crematoria or sparking a larger uprising within the camp, it stands as a testament to the remarkable spirit of resistance and the undying human desire for freedom. The act of defiance by the Sonderkommando was a powerful statement against the Nazi regime, demonstrating that even in the face of certain death, the human spirit could not be completely subdued.

Detailed accounts of this rebellion are documented and displayed in the Auschwitz-Birkenau State Museum. These accounts provide a vivid recounting of their courageous act, highlighting the bravery and resolve of those who chose to fight back against unimaginable oppression. The rebellion is remembered as one of the most significant acts of resistance within the death camps.

The Ovitz Family: The Ovitz family, a Jewish Romanian family, endured the Holocaust with extraordinary strength and unity. Comprising parents Shimson and Brana Ovitz and their ten children, seven of whom were dwarfs and three of average height, they faced persecution and deportation to Auschwitz in 1944. Despite the unimaginable horrors of the concentration camp, the Ovitz family remained remarkably close-knit, providing each other with support and strength. Subjected to medical experiments due to their unique physical characteristics, they endured immense suffering but managed to survive together. Their story of survival and determination, along with their enduring bonds of family, serves as a powerful testament to the human spirit in the face of adversity. The narrative of the Ovitz family is preserved in several Holocaust museums, including Yad Vashem in Israel, ensuring their experiences and resilience are remembered.

The Diary of Anne Frank: Perhaps one of the most famous accounts of survival during the Holocaust, Anne Frank's diary documents her family's two years spent hiding from the Nazis in Amsterdam. Anne's diary captures the spirit of bravery and hope amidst the darkest of times.

Anne Frank was born on June 12, 1929, in Frankfurt, Germany. Her family moved to Amsterdam in 1933, fleeing the increasing persecution of Jews in Nazi Germany. In July 1942, as the Nazis began to deport Jews from the Netherlands, Anne's family went into hiding in a secret annex behind her father's business. Along with the Frank family were four other people, including the Van Pels family and a dentist named Fritz Pfeffer.

For over two years, the eight inhabitants of the annex lived in constant fear of discovery. Despite the dire circumstances, Anne's diary entries reveal a young girl who remained hopeful and introspective. She wrote about her thoughts, fears, and dreams, providing a touching and deeply personal perspective on the impact of war and persecution. Her writings also reflect her growth as a writer and her keen observations of the human condition.

Entry from Anne Frank's Diary

In this photograph is a handwritten note in Dutch, where Anne reflects on her appearance and dreams. The note reads: "This is a photo as I would wish myself to look all the time. Then I might still have a chance to get to Hollywood. But now, I'm afraid I usually look quite different." The note is signed "Anne Frank" with the date "18 Oct. 1942" and location "Amsterdam." This image captures a moment in Anne's life, revealing her youthful aspirations and the reality of her situation as a Jewish girl hiding from Nazi persecution during World War II.
Source: United States Holocaust Memorial Museum.

Anne's diary, which she received as a gift on her 13th birthday, became her confidant and an outlet for her emotions. She wrote about the mundane details of daily life in hiding, the tensions and conflicts within the annex, and her longing for freedom. Her reflections on identity, humanity, and the cruelty of the Nazis offer in depth insights into the struggles of a young girl coming of age in such a turbulent time.

In August 1944, the inhabitants of the secret annex were betrayed and arrested by the Gestapo. Anne and her sister, Margot, were eventually deported to the Bergen-Belsen concentration camp, where they both died of typhus in early 1945, just weeks before the camp was liberated by Allied forces. Anne's father, Otto Frank, was the only member of the family to survive the war. After returning to Amsterdam, he discovered Anne's diary, which had been preserved by one of the family's helpers, Miep Gies. Deeply moved by his daughter's words, Otto decided to fulfill her wish of becoming a published writer. The diary was first published in 1947 under the title "The Diary of a Young Girl."

Anne Frank's diary has since been translated into over 70 languages and remains one of the most widely read books in the world. It serves as a reminder of the human cost of hatred and the enduring spirit of hope in the face of unimaginable adversity. Her diary is displayed in the Anne Frank House in Amsterdam, now a museum dedicated to her memory, and excerpts are also featured in Holocaust exhibits worldwide, providing personal insights into life during the Holocaust and ensuring that her voice continues to resonate with future generations. The museum attracts millions of visitors every year, all drawn by the powerful story of a young girl whose voice became a symbol of courage and the human spirit. Otto Frank's decision to share Anne's words with the world ensures that the lessons of the Holocaust remain vivid and relevant, bridging generations.

Oskar Schindler: A German industrialist and member of the Nazi Party, Oskar Schindler is best known for his extraordinary efforts to save the lives of over 1,200 Jews by employing them in his factories during World War II. His story of bravery and compassion is a remarkable tale of how one man's actions can make a massive difference, even amidst the horrors of the Holocaust.

Born on April 28, 1908, in Zwittau, Moravia (now in the Czech Republic), Schindler was a businessman with a knack for opportunism. When the Nazis invaded Poland in 1939, Schindler moved to Krakow, seizing the opportunity to profit from the war by acquiring a factory that produced enamelware and ammunitions for the German military. It was here, in the Deutsche Emailwarenfabrik (DEF), that Schindler's remarkable transformation began.

Initially motivated by profit, Schindler's perspective changed as he witnessed the brutal treatment of Jews by the Nazis. Employing Jewish workers became more than just a business decision, it became a mission to save lives. Schindler leveraged his connections with high-ranking Nazi officials and his charm to secure contracts and protections for his Jewish workers, who were otherwise destined for the concentration camps. Schindler's list, which included the names of more than 1,200 Jews, was essentially a roster of life. By deeming his workers essential to the war effort, he was able to shield them from deportation and death. Schindler went to great lengths to ensure their safety, even bribing SS officers and providing his workers with extra rations, medical care, and humane working conditions, which were unheard of in other Nazi-operated factories.

Oskar Schindler plants a tree on the Avenue of the Righteous Among the Nations at Yad Vashem. This honor is bestowed upon non-Jewish individuals who, at great personal risk, helped save Jewish lives during the Holocaust. Yad Vashem, Israel's Holocaust memorial, recognizes these brave souls for their extraordinary courage and humanity.

Source: United States Holocaust Memorial Museum.

In October 1944, as the Red Army approached, Schindler managed to move his factory and workers to Brünnlitz in Czechoslovakia. This move was fraught with danger, but Schindler's determination to save his workers never wavered. Despite the war's end approaching, the threat to his worker's lives was still imminent, and Schindler's actions continued to reflect his deep commitment to their survival.

Schindler's efforts were not without personal cost. He expended his entire fortune to protect his Jewish workers and ended the war penniless. After the war, Schindler and his wife Emilie fled to Argentina, where they lived for several years before returning to Germany. Schindler struggled financially and was supported by donations from the grateful Jewish community he had saved.

Schindler's story of courage and compassion was immortalised in the book "Schindler's Ark" by Thomas Keneally, which won the Booker Prize in 1982. The subsequent film adaptation, "Schindler's List," directed by Steven Spielberg in 1993, brought Schindler's heroic deeds to a global audience. The film, which won seven Academy Awards, including Best Picture, depicts Schindler's transformation from a profit-driven businessman to a saviour of Jews during the Holocaust.

In recognition of his extraordinary efforts, Oskar and Emilie Schindler were honoured at Yad Vashem in Israel, where they were named Righteous Among the Nations. This title is given to non-Jews who risked their lives to save Jews during the Holocaust. Their names are inscribed on the Wall of Honour in the Garden of the Righteous, a testament to their bravery and humanity.

The Schindler Factory in Krakow has been converted into a museum, offering insights into his life-saving efforts and the experiences of those he saved. The museum, housed in the original factory building, features exhibits that detail Schindler's efforts, the lives of the Jewish workers, and the broader context of the Holocaust in Krakow. It stands as a powerful reminder of the impact one person can have in the face of evil.

Oskar Schindler's legacy is one of remarkable moral courage and the enduring impact of individual action against systemic evil. His story continues to inspire and remind us of the capacity for goodness and heroism in even the darkest times.

Cultural Preservation: Prisoners in Birkenau secretly preserved their cultural heritage through clandestine artistic activities. Whether it was writing poetry, composing music, or creating visual art, these acts of cultural resistance served as a means of asserting humanity in the face of dehumanisation. This cultural preservation was not just about maintaining a connection to their heritage but also about finding ways to resist the brutal conditions imposed by the Nazis. In some cases, prisoners even created underground newspapers, documenting the horrors they witnessed and sharing messages of hope and defiance Resistance within the shadows of Auschwitz was a courageous act against an orchestrated campaign to rebel against the Nazis. Individuals like the White Rose Group, the Ovitz family, and countless others engaged in acts of defiance, becoming heroes in a landscape tainted by oppression.

Honouring the courage of those who resisted meant recognising that, even in the face of overwhelming power, individuals found ways to assert their dignity. These acts of cultural defiance were often small, such as singing a forbidden song or sharing a piece of poetry, but they carried immense symbolic weight. The clandestine classrooms where education persisted, the secret gatherings where cultural heritage was preserved, and the acts of solidarity that defied the divisions imposed by the oppressors all became monuments to the strength of the human spirit.

Alice Herz-Sommer: Alice Herz-Sommer, a renowned pianist, was the oldest known Holocaust survivor until her passing in 2014 at the age of 110. Born in Prague in 1903, Alice showed an early talent for music, eventually becoming a celebrated concert pianist. Her life took a tragic turn when she was deported to the Theresienstadt (Terezín) concentration camp in 1943 along with her young son, Raphael.

Despite the horrific conditions, Alice's music became a beacon of hope within the camp. She performed over 100 concerts for her fellow prisoners, using her music to lift their spirits and provide a temporary escape from the daily horrors. Her performances were a testament to the enduring power of art and its ability to bring comfort and hope even in the darkest of times. After the war, Alice and Raphael were liberated, and she continued her musical career, eventually moving to Israel and then to London. Her remarkable story of survival and the role of music in sustaining her spirit during the Holocaust is chronicled in the Oscar-winning documentary "The Lady in Number 6: Music Saved My Life." Her legacy continues to inspire and remind us of the enduring power of art to overcome adversity.

Elie Wiesel: Among the countless stories of survival and resistance within Auschwitz, few have resonated as powerfully as that of Elie Wiesel. Born in 1928 in the town of Sighet, Romania, Wiesel was only 15 years old when his life was irrevocably altered. In 1944, he and his family were deported to Auschwitz-Birkenau. Upon arrival at Auschwitz, the Wiesel family was torn apart. Elie was separated from his mother and younger sister, both of whom he would never see again. He and his father, Shlomo, were selected for forced labor, a decision that condemned them to the brutal realities of the camp. The bond between father and son became a lifeline in the face of relentless dehumanization, as they clung to each other for strength and hope. Life in Auschwitz was a daily battle for survival. Wiesel endured the constant threat of death, the loss of his loved ones, and the erosion of his faith. The horrors he witnessed, the gas chambers, the crematoria, the endless suffering, left an indelible mark on his soul. The father and son duo faced the brutality of the camp guards, the starvation, and the bitter cold together, but their shared struggle only deepened the despair. As the Soviet army advanced in January 1945, the Nazis evacuated Auschwitz, forcing Wiesel and his father on a death march to Buchenwald. The journey was excruciating, with many prisoners succumbing to the cold and exhaustion. In Buchenwald, Wiesel's father grew increasingly weak, and in early 1945, Shlomo Wiesel died, leaving his son utterly alone. Liberation came in April 1945, but the wounds of Wiesel's experiences ran deep. He was orphaned, and got physically weak. For years, Wiesel remained silent about his ordeal, grappling with the overwhelming pain and the questions that lingered in his heart. It wasn't until 1956 that Wiesel began to share his story with the world. His memoir, *"Night,"* is a haunting account of his experiences in Auschwitz and Buchenwald. Written with an honesty, *"Night"* captures the raw anguish of a young boy who witnessed the depths of human cruelty and survived against all odds. The book quickly became one of the most important testimonies of the Holocaust, offering readers a deeply personal and universally significant perspective on the atrocities of the time. Elie Wiesel's story did not end with his survival, it continued as he became one of the most vocal advocates for Holocaust remembrance and human rights. In 1986, he was awarded the Nobel Peace Prize, a recognition of his tireless efforts to ensure that the world never forgets the lessons of the Holocaust. Wiesel's life tell us that survival is not just about living through an ordeal, it is about finding meaning and purpose in the aftermath. His experiences in Auschwitz shaped him into a voice for the voiceless and a guardian of memory.

These tales of resistance were not mere historical footnotes, they were reminders that even in the darkest corners of history, the flame of resistance could never be fully extinguished. Honouring the courage of those who resisted became a commitment to carry forward the legacy of defiance, ensuring that their stories would continue to inspire generations to come.

In the middle of the harrowing narratives of loss and suffering, stories of survival within Auschwitz emerged as beacons of hope. Each survivor became a living testament to the triumph of the human will over the machinery of death. Finding inspiration in these stories meant acknowledging the hope over despair. The survivors, sharing their experiences with raw vulnerability, became sources of inspiration that transformed historical interpretation. Their ability to rebuild their lives, to find purpose in the aftermath of unimaginable loss, spoke to the irrepressible human spirit. In their resilience, I found inspiration to withstand adversity, to stand against injustice, and to foster a world where these ghastly acts of Auschwitz would not be repeated.

As I delved into the stories of survival and resistance within Auschwitz, the chapter unfolded as a tapestry woven with threads of human fortitude. It became a testament to the enduring flame of hope, an acknowledgment that even in the darkest chapters of history, stories of resilience and resistance could illuminate the path forward. The journey through the camp was not just a reckoning with the past, it was an affirmation of the enduring strength of the human spirit, a commitment to honour the courage of those who resisted, and a pledge to draw inspiration from the indomitable will to survive.

Image captured by the author ©

This photograph captures a window display outside Oskar Schindler's Factory. The window is filled with a mosaic of black-and-white portraits, each representing individuals saved by Schindler during the Holocaust. The expressions captured in these portraits convey a range of emotions, from solemnity to hope, offering a deeply personal glimpse into the lives that were spared due to one man's extraordinary bravery and humanity.

Image captured by the author ©

This photograph captures a commemorative plaque installed at the Schindler Factory, now a museum in Krakow, Poland. The plaque honours Oskar Schindler, a German industrialist who saved over 1,200 Jews during the Holocaust by employing them in his enamelware and ammunitions factories. The plaque is inscribed with a quote from the Talmud Yerushalmi, Sanhedrin 4:12: "Whoever saves one life, saves the world entire."

Image captured by the author ©

This photograph features a historical image displayed at Auschwitz 1, depicting a group of prisoners standing behind barbed wire, moments after liberation. The expressions on their faces convey a mixture of relief, bewilderment, and lingering fear, capturing a powerful moment of transition from captivity to freedom. Their haggard faces and gaunt bodies are a testament to the suffering and deprivation they endured. It serves not only to honour the victims and survivors of Auschwitz but also to ensure that future generations understand the depths of human cruelty and the enduring strength of the human spirit.

CHAPTER 9
AFTER THE WAR

The aftermath of World War II cast a long shadow over Auschwitz, forever altering its landscape. What was once a site of unspeakable horror began its transformation into a place of remembrance and education. On January 27, 1945, when the Soviet Red Army liberated Auschwitz, the camp's grim secrets started to unravel. This moment marked the beginning of a crucial period – one focused on documenting atrocities, caring for survivors, prosecuting the guilty, and preserving the memory of the Holocaust.

Liberation and Immediate Aftermath: As Soviet troops entered Auschwitz, they found around 7,000 prisoners who had miraculously survived, though most were skeletal and desperately ill. The soldiers discovered the mountains of corpses, piles of abandoned belongings, and the crumbling remains of the camp. The first priority was clear, care for those who had endured unimaginable suffering. Field hospitals sprang up, and frantic attempts were made to reunite families, though many would remain forever separated by the vast chasm of loss. The sight of the survivors, emaciated and weak, underscored the horrors they had endured. Medical teams worked tirelessly to save lives, battling malnutrition, disease, and the psychological scars of trauma. Simultaneously, the liberators embarked on the task of documenting the horrors they discovered. They took photographs, collected testimonies, and gathered physical evidence, determined to make sure the world understood the full extent of the Nazi crimes. Soviet and Allied forces meticulously recorded the conditions of the camp, the testimonies of survivors, and the physical evidence of mass murder. This effort was crucial in ensuring that the atrocities were not denied or forgotten. This painstaking documentation would later prove indispensable during the Nuremberg Trials, ensuring that justice could be pursued.

Trials of War Criminals: The Nuremberg Trials, which took place from 1945 to 1946, were the most prominent prosecutions of Nazi war criminals, yet they were far from the only ones. Specific trials, such as those for the crimes committed at Auschwitz, brought many of the camp's perpetrators to justice. Among the most notorious was Rudolf Höss, the commandant of Auschwitz. Captured by the British in March 1946, Höss provided chillingly detailed testimony about the camp's operations, admitting to the mass murder of millions. His testimony was a key piece in the grim puzzle of the Holocaust. Convicted of war crimes and crimes against humanity, Höss was executed by hanging in 1947 as shown on *Page 116*. The trials served not only as a means of justice but also as a critical historical record, affirming the scale and intentionality of the Holocaust. The Auschwitz Trial in Krakow, starting on November 24, 1947, was another significant moment. It saw 40 former SS members and kapos (prisoner functionaries) of Auschwitz stand trial. High-ranking officers like Arthur Liebehenschel, Maria Mandel, and Hans Aumeier were among the defendants. The trial revealed harrowing details about daily life and death in the camp. Out of the 40 defendants, 23 were sentenced to death, while others received various prison terms. Additionally, these trials underscored the importance of international cooperation in bringing perpetrators to justice, as judges were selected from Allied countries, and the trials were conducted under the auspices of international law. The careful documentation and testimonies collected during these trials also played a crucial role in dispelling any attempts at Holocaust denial, ensuring that the evidence of these atrocities was irrefutable. While many Nazis were convicted, some fled justice, with several high-ranking officials, such as Adolf Eichmann and Josef Mengele, escaping to Argentina and other South American countries. The hunt for these fugitives continued for decades, with figures like Eichmann eventually being captured, tried, and executed, while others, like Mengele, evaded capture until their deaths. These trials were vital in holding individuals accountable and ensuring that the atrocities were formally recognised and condemned. The legal precedents set by these trials also laid the groundwork for future international human rights law, including the Genocide Convention and the establishment of the International Criminal Court.

Preservation as a Historical Site: In the years after the war, a consensus emerged, Auschwitz must be preserved. In 1947, the Polish government founded the Auschwitz-Birkenau State Museum. This institution was charged with maintaining the site and educating visitors about the Holocaust. The preservation efforts involved not only maintaining the physical structures but also curating an extensive collection of artifacts, documents, and personal belongings of the victims. The aim was to create a comprehensive historical record that future generations could learn from. Efforts were meticulous, focusing on maintaining the barracks, gas chambers, crematoria, and other structures to ensure future generations could witness these physical remnants of horror. The museum also curated personal items left behind by the victims, such as, shoes, suitcases, eyeglasses etc. These artifacts, displayed in carefully designed exhibits, serve as reminders of the lives lost.

Memorials and Commemorations: Over the years, numerous memorials have been erected at Auschwitz to honour the victims. The International Monument to the Victims of Fascism, unveiled in 1967, stands as the most significant of these. Located between the ruins of crematoria II and III, this monument features plaques in multiple languages, each bearing the inscription, "For ever let this place be a cry of despair and a warning to humanity." Annual commemorations, such as International Holocaust Remembrance Day on January 27, see survivors, their families, dignitaries, and the public gather to honour the victims. These events are marked by speeches, moments of silence, and the lighting of candles. They are designed to foster a collective memory of the Holocaust and reinforce the global commitment to preventing future genocides. In addition to these formal events, there are educational programs and initiatives that involve younger generations. These programs often include guided tours, survivor testimonies, and interactive exhibits that deepen the understanding of the Holocaust's impact.

In the end, the transformation of Auschwitz from a place of suffering to a site of memory underscores the crucial need to remember. The efforts to care for survivors, prosecute war criminals, and preserve the site ensure that the lessons of the Holocaust will endure, a reminder to future generations of the depths of human cruelty and the enduring need for vigilance.

Image captured by the author ©

This photograph depicts one of the many memorial tablets, each of them in a different European language, which are present at the Auschwitz-Birkenau (II) monument. The plaque solemnly declares, "For ever let this place be a cry of despair and a warning to humanity, where the Nazis murdered about one and a half million men, women, and children, mainly Jews from various countries of Europe." The silent presence of this memorial ensures that the voices of those lost are never forgotten.

This photograph depicts a vast, open field bordered by barbed wire fences supported by sturdy wooden posts, a characteristic feature of the camp's perimeter of Auschwitz II-Birkenau. The oppressive atmosphere is accentuated by the heavy, overcast sky above. In the distance, remnants of structures can be seen, the foundations of barracks or other camp facilities, hinting at the extensive and harrowing history of the site.

CHAPTER 10
THE ROLE OF REMEMBRANCE

In the realm of Auschwitz, the act of remembrance emerges as a vital duty, not just to the millions of souls who met their tragic fate within its confines, but to the shared conscience of humanity. As I contemplate the significance of memorialisation, the responsibility to bear witness takes hold, and the imperative to link the past with present issues becomes an undeniable call to action. Memorialisation within Auschwitz extends beyond physical monuments or commemorative plaques. It becomes a living, breathing entity, an unwritten pact to ensure that the stories etched into these sacred grounds won't fade into the forgotten recesses of history.

The true significance lies in transforming the remnants of atrocity into pillars of remembrance, forging a collective commitment to honour the lives lost and to bear witness to the unimaginable suffering endured. Remembering and honouring the past creates the heartbreaking canvas of scattered shoes, the gas chambers, and the resilient voices of survivors converging to create an immersive experience. It's a deliberate effort to preserve the past, not as a distant memory, but as a living testament. The stories of Auschwitz are not just relics of a foregone era, they are intertwined with the essence of our shared humanity, serving as powerful reminders of our capacity for both good and evil.

Bearing witness to the atrocities of Auschwitz amplifies the role of passive observers. It's an active engagement with history.

The responsibility of bearing witness isn't a mere formality, it's a solemn vow to ensure that the stories of Auschwitz remain vivid, visceral, and undiminished by the passage of time.

To bear witness is to deal with uncomfortable truths, listen to the testimonies of survivors, and recognise the human capacity for both darkness and light. It's an invitation to stand at the intersection of past and present, acknowledging the sins of history and resolving to prevent their recurrence. This responsibility carries a weight, a weight that fuels the commitment to act as custodians of memory, ensuring that the lessons learned from Auschwitz resonate through generations. Real recorded incidents underscore the significance of remembrance. Survivors stories, such as those of Elie Wiesel and Primo Levi, become living testimonials to the resilience of the human spirit. Their narratives, often marked by acts of solidarity and resistance, illuminate the importance of bearing witness to prevent the erasure of these stories from our collective consciousness.

The echoes of Auschwitz aren't confined to the past, they reverberate through the corridors of contemporary issues. The act of remembrance carries an inherent responsibility to draw connections between historical atrocities and present day challenges. It's an imperative to recognise warning signs, mitigate the roots of prejudice and hatred, and actively participate in dismantling the structures that enable genocide.

Connecting the past to contemporary issues means acknowledging that the lessons of Auschwitz aren't restricted to a specific time or place. They are universal truths that go past borders, cultures, and generations. It's an understanding that the fight against injustice, discrimination, and dehumanisation is an ongoing struggle. A struggle that demands collective vigilance, and a commitment to building a world where the shadows of Auschwitz hold no sway. In today's world, we see the resurgence of hate crimes, xenophobia, and extremist ideologies. The lessons of Auschwitz remind us of the dangers of allowing such sentiments to fester unchecked. As I reflect on the role of remembrance, the responsibility of bearing witness, and the imperative to connect the past to contemporary issues, I realise that Auschwitz is not merely a historical chapter but a living testament to the fragility of humanity and the resilience of the human spirit. The journey through its grounds becomes a transformative experience. It compels us to address contemporary issues such as racism, Anti-Semitism, and other forms of bigotry with the seriousness they deserve. A journey not only into the heart of darkness but towards a future illuminated by the lessons learned.

Educational programs, like those at the United States Holocaust Memorial Museum and Yad Vashem, play a crucial role in keeping the memory of Auschwitz alive while applying its lessons to the present. By educating new generations about the horrors of the Holocaust, these institutions foster an understanding of the importance of combating hate and promoting tolerance.

Reflecting on the importance of remembrance, I am reminded that it is not a passive act but an active commitment to justice and humanity. In remembering Auschwitz, we are called to build a world where such atrocities are impossible, where the dignity of every individual is upheld, and where the values of souls and understanding triumph over hatred and division.

Image captured by the author ©

The 'Piłsudski Bridge' in Kraków city near Auschwitz-Birkenau, Poland, is a historic bridge spanning the Vistula River, notable for its architectural significance and its role during World War II. Constructed between 1926 and 1933, it became a crucial part of the city's infrastructure. During the Holocaust, the bridge was a witness to the forced movements of Jews into the Kraków ghetto and their subsequent deportations to extermination camps such as Auschwitz.

Page 115

Image captured by the author ©

This photograph captures the execution site at Auschwitz I. During the camp's operation, this gallows was used for public executions, often intended to instil fear among the prisoners. Executions were carried out as punishment for various offences, including attempts to escape or acts of resistance against the Nazi regime. The most notable execution was that of Rudolf Höss, the former commandant of Auschwitz, who was sentenced to death and hanged here in 1947 after being convicted of war crimes and crimes against humanity.

Image captured by the author ©

This evocative photograph captures a solitary cattle car on the railway tracks inside the premises of Auschwitz II-Birkenau, under a brooding sky. The isolated image of the train car, with the watchtower in the background, evokes the memories of the countless deportations that took place during the Holocaust. These cattle cars, often produced by companies such as Deutsche Reichsbahn, were used to transport millions of Jews and other victims to their grim fates, often under horrific conditions, crammed together without food, water, or sanitation for days.

CHAPTER 11
LESSONS FOR TODAY

As I wrap up my visit to this camp, almost the whole day is spent pondering on the past, present and future. I am struck by the valuable lessons it holds for our world today. The experience has given me much to think about regarding the challenges of our time, but let's dive into these insights.

To visit Auschwitz is to engage with the painful past, to bear witness to the atrocities committed at this place, and to reaffirm our commitment to never again allow such horrors to unfold. Beyond its historical importance, Auschwitz serves as a catalyst for reflection and introspection. It compels us to examine the darker recesses of our own humanity, to confront the prejudices and biases that still linger in our societies today. It reminds us that the seeds of hatred, once sown, can flourish into unspeakable violence if left unchecked. The lessons of Auschwitz underscore the dangers of indifference and the necessity of vigilance in safeguarding human rights.

Auschwitz, rather than just a relic of the past, serves as a reminder of the problems we still face today. Its lessons go beyond history books, guiding us towards a future filled with apprehension and a commitment to keeping our world bright. One of the most pressing contemporary lessons from Auschwitz is the importance of combating hate speech and extremist ideologies. In today's digital age, these dangerous ideas can spread rapidly through social media and online platforms, reaching a global audience. It is imperative that we counteract this by promoting messages of tolerance, togetherness, and inclusivity. Educational programs that teach the history of the Holocaust and other genocides can help inoculate younger generations against the lure of extremist rhetoric.

Considering Auschwitz's relevance today, I can't help but see its lessons in the world around us. Hate crimes are on the rise, extreme ideologies are making a comeback, and discrimination still lingers. It's a wake-up call that we can't ignore these warnings from history. Auschwitz underscores the dangers of indifference and complicity in the face of injustice. The Holocaust did not occur in a vacuum, it was facilitated by the apathy and accession of ordinary individuals who chose to turn a blind eye to the suffering of their fellow human beings. In today's world, where injustices continue to mushroom, Auschwitz compels us to face our own complicity and to take a stand against hatred and oppression wherever it may arise. This includes speaking out against discriminatory policies, supporting marginalized communities, and actively participating in the democratic process to ensure that the rights of all individuals are protected.

Moreover, Auschwitz serves as a record against the dangers of demonising the "other" and perpetuating degrading ideologies. The dehumanisation of Jews, Roma , LGBTQ+ individuals, and other marginalised groups paved the way for their extermination. Today, as we witness the re-emergence of xenophobia, racism, and extremism, Auschwitz serves as a warning of the consequences of intolerance and prejudice. It is essential that we challenge these ideologies whenever and wherever they arise, promoting a culture of acceptance and understanding.

The Holocaust teaches us about the critical importance of preserving democratic institutions and protecting human rights. The erosion of democratic norms and the rise of authoritarian regimes are often precursors to mass atrocities. By strengthening democratic values, ensuring the rule of law, and protecting the rights of minorities, we can create societies that are resilient against the forces of hatred and division. This place isn't just a static piece of history, it's a living reminder of what can happen when we let hatred and indifference take over. Its modern significance is like a moral compass, pointing us to take responsibility for the injustices and prejudices that still exist. The lessons from Auschwitz call us to actively resist hatred, discrimination, and indifference. We can see this in real-time examples like the efforts to challenge bias or promote diversity and inclusion. It's about shaking up the norm and creating spaces where everyone feels welcome.

Hatred, as we've seen from Auschwitz, doesn't pop up overnight, it starts with indifference. Our commitment to fighting it should go beyond just opposing big acts of discrimination. It's also about breaking down the subtle biases that exist in our everyday lives. This involves self-reflection and a willingness to challenge our own prejudices. It also means fostering environments where open dialogue and mutual respect are encouraged.

Auschwitz highlights the importance of fostering awareness and compassion in our interactions with others. In a world filled with division and conflicts, it calls upon us to cultivate sensitivity to recognise the inherent dignity and worth of every individual, and to strive towards a more compassionate and inclusive society. Acts of kindness and understanding, no matter how small, contribute to a broader culture of tolerance that can counteract the forces of hatred. Additionally, the role of education cannot be overstated. By integrating the lessons of the Holocaust into school curricula worldwide, we can equip future generations with the knowledge and moral framework needed to prevent such atrocities. Educational initiatives should not only focus on the historical facts but also on the ethical and moral lessons that arise from the Holocaust.

In today's world, these insights encourage us to educate, foster awareness, and promote inclusivity. Real-time examples, like initiatives challenging systemic biases, show that Auschwitz's lessons are still relevant. We need to actively be part of building up societies where such evil deeds are replaced by understanding and acceptance. I'm taking away lessons that are more than just historical facts. They're a guide to making our future brighter, with compassion and justice leading the way. Moreover, the establishment and support of institutions dedicated to human rights and genocide prevention are critical. Organisations like the United Nations, the International Criminal Court, and various non-governmental organisations work tirelessly to monitor and address potential human rights abuses around the world. Supporting these institutions and their missions is a vital part of applying the lessons of Auschwitz to contemporary global issues.

My journey through Auschwitz isn't just about looking into the past, it's an invitation to contribute to a future filled with kindness, fairness, and a commitment to making sure the shadows of Auschwitz stay in the past. My departure from Auschwitz isn't just about leaving the past behind, but also learning from them. This commitment involves continuous education, advocacy for human rights, and active participation in efforts to create inclusive and just societies.

In this chapter, it is essential to highlight positive examples of how communities are applying these lessons today. One such initiative is the **Sisterhood of Salaam Shalom,** an organisation that fosters relationships between Muslim and Jewish women to combat hate and promote mutual understanding. By creating a platform for dialogue, these women break down barriers of prejudice and build bridges of empathy and solidarity. Their work is a testament to the power of grassroots efforts in fostering peace and understanding in a divided world.The Sisterhood of Salaam Shalom goes beyond just fostering dialogue, it also engages in joint social action projects, educational events, and advocacy efforts that empower women to stand together against all forms of discrimination and injustice. Founded by Sheryl Olitzky and Atiya Aftab in 2010, the organization has grown to include dozens of chapters across North America. Members of the Sisterhood participate in activities ranging from sharing personal stories and religious practices to collaborating on community service projects that benefit those in need. They also participate in annual retreats, which offer opportunities for deeper connection and understanding through workshops, discussions, and shared cultural experiences. Through these shared experiences, the Sisterhood builds lasting relationships and dismantles stereotypes, demonstrating how unity and understanding can effectively counteract the divisiveness of hatred and prejudice.Their work has received recognition and support from various communities, showcasing how interfaith efforts can pave the way for broader societal change. This organization exemplifies how grassroots efforts can lead to meaningful social change, contributing to a more inclusive and compassionate world.

Another inspiring example is the **Global Network of Memory Sites**, which includes institutions like the United States Holocaust Memorial Museum and Yad Vashem. These organisations work tirelessly to educate the public about the Holocaust and other genocides, ensuring that the lessons of the past are not forgotten. Through exhibitions, educational programs, and survivor testimonies, they keep the memory of Auschwitz alive, reminding us of our collective responsibility to prevent such atrocities in the future. The Global Network of Memory Sites also fosters international cooperation by connecting various museums, memorials, and educational institutions worldwide. This collaboration enhances the sharing of resources, research, and best practices, thereby amplifying the impact of Holocaust education globally. For example, Yad Vashem's "Shoah Victims' Names Recovery Project" partners with communities around the world to ensure that the names of Holocaust victims are preserved, while the United States Holocaust Memorial Museum's leadership in the Genocide Prevention Task Force exemplifies its commitment to preventing future atrocities.These initiatives and countless others around the world embody the enduring lessons of Auschwitz. They demonstrate that, through education, consideration, and active engagement, we can combat hatred and build a more inclusive and compassionate world. As we carry these lessons forward, we honour the memory of those who suffered and ensure that their stories continue to inspire positive change.

In the end, the echoes of Auschwitz are a call to action. They remind us that we must remain vigilant against the forces of hatred and intolerance and commit ourselves to building a future where such darkness has no place. This is the enduring legacy of Auschwitz, and it is a legacy that we must carry forward with determination and hope. By actively applying the lessons of Auschwitz to our daily lives and the broader societal context, we contribute to a world that honours the memory of those who suffered.

Image captured by the author ©

This photograph features a window from the Auschwitz-Birkenau State Museum, specifically from an exhibition titled "The Citizen Betrayed – To the Memory of the Hungarian Holocaust." The sign on the window, written in both Polish and English, signifies an exhibition dedicated to remembering the Hungarian Jews who were deported to Auschwitz during the Holocaust. The exhibit housed within this structure aims to educate visitors about the specific experiences and tragic fate of Hungarian Jews who were among the millions of victims of the Nazi genocide. The exhibit serves to honour their memory and educate future generations about the importance of tolerance and remembrance.

This photograph captures an informational display at Auschwitz II-Birkenau, detailing the history and functions of the gas chamber and crematorium II. The image at the top of the display shows the exterior of the crematorium building as it stood during the camp's operation, surrounded by a desolate landscape. It tells several hundred thousand Jews, Roma, and other victims were murdered by gas and later had their bodies burned in this very facility. The display provides a chilling account of the systematic extermination process, emphasising the sheer scale of the atrocities committed.

Page 125

This photograph captures the entrance gate to the female camp side at Auschwitz II-Birkenau. The gate, composed of metal and wood, stands as a symbol of the confinement and suffering experienced by the women imprisoned here. The barbed wire and electrified fencing surrounding the gate underscore the oppressive nature of the camp, designed to prevent escape and enforce control. The symmetrical design of the gate, with its crisscrossed metal bars and locked doors, conveys a sense of finality and entrapment.

Conclusion: Echoes that Endure

As I conclude this visit, a sense of responsibility lingers, a duty to carry forward the stories of Auschwitz, to educate others about the past, and to stand against hatred and indifference. The enduring echoes of this place call for a commitment to shape a world where the mistakes of history are acknowledged and not repeated. The lessons learned from Auschwitz are not relics of the past, they serve as beacons guiding us through the challenges of today. It calls us to engage in building a world where the sorrowful legacy of Auschwitz gives rise to a culture of mutual respect and kindness.

Leaving Auschwitz doesn't mark the end of this journey, it sparks a newfound motivation within me. I feel compelled to contribute to ongoing conversations about remembrance, tolerance, and the importance of upholding human dignity. This visit inspires me to be a vigilant keeper of memory and an advocate for a future where history's lessons are not forgotten. Stepping away from Auschwitz, my commitment to combat injustice and discrimination remains resolute. This journey, both haunting and hopeful, propels me towards a future where the lessons learned from history guide us to a world characterised by an unwavering commitment to ensure that the echoes of Auschwitz persist, bearing witness to the resilience of the human spirit.

The journey to Auschwitz is a deeply personal and incredibly transformative experience. It is a journey of remembrance, of understanding, and of bearing witness to the darkest depths of human history. To visit Auschwitz is to confront the past, to honour the memory of the millions who perished, and to reaffirm our commitment to building a future free from hatred and intolerance. The atmosphere of Auschwitz serves as a reminder of the fragility of human rights and the ease with which they can be stripped away under oppressive regimes. The physical remnants of the camp, its barracks, gas chambers, and crematoria stand as solemn witnesses to the atrocities committed. They challenge visitors to reflect deeply on the consequences of unchecked hatred and prejudice.

As I walk away from this place, I am reminded that remembrance is not passive. It is an active process that requires us to face the uncomfortable truths, engage in difficult conversations, and educate others about the past. The stories of those who suffered here demand our attention and our action. They compel us to foster a culture of tolerance, care and respect for human dignity. This experience has reinforced my belief in the power of education and dialogue in preventing future atrocities. By learning from the past and teaching future generations about the horrors of the Holocaust, we can work towards a world where such events are never repeated.

KEY DATES

- April 27, 1940 – Heinrich Himmler Orders the Establishment of Auschwitz - Heinrich Himmler, head of the SS, orders the establishment of a concentration camp in the Polish town of Oświęcim, which the Germans rename Auschwitz. Originally intended to house Polish political prisoners, Auschwitz I becomes the core of a vast complex of labor, concentration, and extermination camps.

- May 20, 1940 – First Group of Prisoners Arrives -The first transport of 30 German criminals arrives at Auschwitz I to serve as functionaries and oversee the camp's operations. This marks the beginning of Auschwitz's role as a center of forced labor and imprisonment.

- June 14, 1940 – First Transport of Polish Political Prisoners The first transport of 728 Polish political prisoners arrives at Auschwitz I. These prisoners are subjected to brutal labor and inhumane conditions, marking the camp's transformation into a site of mass persecution.

- July 6, 1940 – First Execution in Auschwitz - The first execution in Auschwitz is carried out. A group of Polish prisoners is shot by SS guards, setting a precedent for the brutal methods that will become routine in the camp.

- March 1, 1941 – Expansion Plans for Auschwitz - Reichsführer-SS Heinrich Himmler visits Auschwitz and orders its expansion to hold 30,000 prisoners. This expansion includes the construction of Auschwitz II-Birkenau, which will later become the primary extermination site.

- September 3, 1941 – First Gassing Experiments SS officials conduct the first gassing experiments at Auschwitz, using Zyklon B on 600 Soviet POWs and 250 ill Polish inmates. This marks the beginning of Auschwitz's transformation into a center for mass murder.

- October 1941 – Construction of Auschwitz II-Birkenau Begins. The Nazis begin construction of Auschwitz II-Birkenau, designed as the largest of the Auschwitz camps. Birkenau is intended as a death camp, equipped with gas chambers and crematoria for the systematic murder of Jews and other targeted groups.

* January 25, 1942 - Himmler Orders the Deportation of Jews to Auschwitz. Heinrich Himmler orders the deportation of Jews to Auschwitz as part of the Nazis' "Final Solution." This order expands Auschwitz's role from a labor camp to a central site of the Holocaust's genocide.

* February 15, 1942 – First Mass Transport of Jews to Auschwitz - The first mass transport of Jews arrives at Auschwitz II-Birkenau, signalling the start of the camp's function as a major site of extermination.

* March 1942 – Mass Extermination Begins at Auschwitz II-Birkenau - Auschwitz II-Birkenau begins operating as a death camp. Trains carrying Jews, Romani people, Soviet POWs, and others arrive daily. Most are sent directly to gas chambers, marking the start of industrial-scale genocide at Auschwitz.

* July 17-22, 1942 – Deportations from the Warsaw Ghetto to Auschwitz- The Nazis begin large-scale deportations from the Warsaw Ghetto to Auschwitz. This is part of the broader effort to deport Jews from ghettos across Europe to extermination camps.

* February 26, 1943 – Arrival of Roma Families at Auschwitz- The first transport of Roma (Gypsies) from Germany arrives at Auschwitz-Birkenau, where families are housed together in Section B-IIe, known as the "Gypsy camp." Over the course of 1943, more than 18,000 Roma are incarcerated here. Ultimately, around 23,000 Roma are deported to Auschwitz, with approximately 21,000 perishing in gas chambers or succumbing to starvation and disease within the brutal confines of the camp.

* September 1943 – Liquidation of the Krakow Ghetto - The Nazis liquidate the Krakow Ghetto, deporting the remaining Jewish residents to Auschwitz-Birkenau, where most are immediately killed in gas chambers. This marks the destruction of one of the last major Jewish communities in Poland.

- May 2, 1944 – First Transport of Hungarian Jews Arrives: The first two transports of Hungarian Jews arrive at Auschwitz-Birkenau. This marks the beginning of the largest and most rapid mass deportation to the camp. Over the next two months, nearly 440,000 Hungarian Jews are deported, with the vast majority sent directly to the gas chambers. This period represents the peak of Auschwitz's function.

- October 7, 1944 – Jewish Prisoners Revolt - Jewish prisoners working in Auschwitz-Birkenau's crematoria stage a revolt, destroying one of the crematoria. Although the uprising is quickly crushed, it stands as a symbol of resistance against the Nazis.

- November 1944 – Cease of Mass Gassings - As the Allies advance and the end of the war looms, the Nazis order a halt to mass gassings at Auschwitz II-Birkenau. The remaining prisoners are forced on death marches to other camps in Germany, as the SS tries to erase evidence of their crimes.

- January 18, 1945 – Evacuation and Death Marches - In the face of the approaching Soviet army, the SS begins evacuating Auschwitz, forcing approximately 60,000 prisoners on death marches toward camps in Germany. Thousands perish due to starvation, exhaustion, and brutality.

- January 27, 1945 – Liberation of Auschwitz - The Soviet Red Army liberates the Auschwitz concentration camp complex. The soldiers find approximately 7,500 survivors, many of whom are gravely ill. This date becomes a symbol of the end of the Nazi genocide and the horrors of the Holocaust.

- May 7-8, 1945 – End of World War II in Europe - Germany surrenders to the Allies, officially bringing an end to the war in Europe. The Holocaust leaves an indelible mark on history, with Auschwitz standing as a primary symbol of Nazi atrocities.

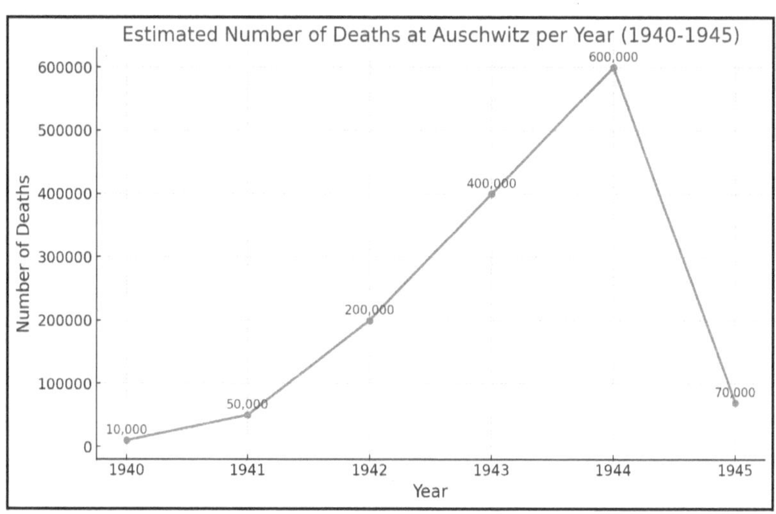

The graph depicting the estimated number of deaths at Auschwitz from 1940 to 1945 offers a visual representation of the estimated number of deaths in the camp. Beginning with the camp's establishment in May 1940, the graph shows a gradual increase in deaths as the Nazis expanded Auschwitz from a detention center for Polish political prisoners to a sprawling complex of forced labor and extermination camps. The graph illustrates the sharp rise in killings starting in 1942, coinciding with the implementation of the "Final Solution." This year marks the point when Auschwitz II-Birkenau became fully operational as a death camp. The deaths peak in 1944, the deadliest year, largely due to the deportation of hundreds of thousands of Hungarian Jews. The graph shows an escalation as the Nazis, desperate to carry out their genocidal goals before the impending Allied advance, intensified their extermination efforts.

By 1945, as the Soviet Army approached, the graph shows a steep decline in deaths, reflecting the cessation of mass gassings and the beginning of the camp's evacuation. However, the graph also underscores that even in the final days, the killing did not completely stop, thousands still perished during the death marches or in the final brutal acts within the camp.

GLOSSARY

Allied Forces: The coalition of nations, including the United States, United Kingdom, Soviet Union, and others, that fought against the Axis powers during World War II.

Arbeit Macht Frei: A German phrase meaning "Work sets you free," infamously placed at the entrances of several Nazi concentration camps, including Auschwitz, to deceive prisoners about their fate.

Auschwitz-Birkenau: A complex of concentration and extermination camps operated by Nazi Germany in occupied Poland during World War II, where over a million people were murdered.

Anti-Semitism: Hostility to, prejudice against, or discrimination against Jews as a religious, ethnic, or racial group, which was a driving force behind the atrocities committed during the Holocaust.

Axis Powers: The alliance of Germany, Italy, and Japan, along with other nations, that opposed the Allied Forces during World War II.

Bergen-Belsen: A Nazi concentration camp in Germany where many prisoners, including Anne Frank, died due to disease and starvation. It was liberated by British forces in 1945.

Birkenau: Also known as Auschwitz II, this was the largest of the Auschwitz camps and served as a primary site for the mass murder of Jews and others in gas chambers.

Crematorium: A facility in Auschwitz used for burning the bodies of those who were killed in gas chambers or died from other causes.

Einsatzgruppen: Mobile killing units of the Nazi SS responsible for mass shootings, primarily of Jews, during the Holocaust.

Euthanasia: A term appropriated by the Nazis to describe their policy of systematically murdering individuals they deemed "life unworthy of life," including the disabled, mentally ill, and others.

Final Solution: The Nazi plan for the genocide of the Jewish people during World War II, resulting in the systematic extermination of six million Jews.

Gestapo: The official secret police of Nazi Germany and German-occupied Europe, notorious for its brutal methods and enforcement of Nazi policies.

Gas Chamber: A sealed chamber used by the Nazis to kill large numbers of people with poisonous gas, primarily Zyklon B, as part of the Holocaust's extermination process.

Genocide: The deliberate and systematic destruction of a racial, political, or cultural group. The Holocaust is one of the most infamous examples of genocide in history.

Ghetto: A section of a city where Jews were forcibly confined during World War II by the Nazis. The ghettos were overcrowded, with poor living conditions, and were often used as holding areas before Jews were deported to concentration camps. Ghettos symbolized the segregation, oppression, and dehumanization that were central to Nazi ideology during the Holocaust. Notable examples include the Warsaw Ghetto and the Krakow Ghetto, where horrific conditions led to widespread death from starvation, disease, and mass executions.

Holocaust: The genocide of six million Jews, along with millions of others, including Roma, disabled individuals, political prisoners, and others, by Nazi Germany during World War II.

Kapo: A prisoner in a Nazi concentration camp who was assigned by the SS guards to supervise forced labor or carry out administrative tasks.

Kristallnacht: Also known as the "Night of Broken Glass," this was a pogrom against Jews carried out by SA paramilitary forces and civilians throughout Nazi Germany on November 9-10, 1938, marked by the destruction of Jewish homes, businesses, and synagogues.

Liberation: The process of freeing the concentration camps, which began in 1944 and continued until the end of World War II in 1945, when Allied forces liberated the surviving prisoners.

Mengele, Josef: A Nazi doctor at Auschwitz, infamous for conducting inhumane medical experiments, especially on twins. Known as the "Angel of Death," his experiments caused severe suffering and death.

Nazi: A member of the National Socialist German Workers' Party, the political party led by Adolf Hitler that ruled Germany from 1933 to 1945 and was responsible for initiating World War II and carrying out the Holocaust.

Nuremberg Trials: A series of military tribunals held after World War II to prosecute prominent leaders of Nazi Germany. The trials were notable for the prosecution of crimes against humanity, including the Holocaust.

Operation 1005: A Nazi operation aimed at erasing the evidence of mass murder by exhuming and burning bodies from mass graves.

Resistance: The various efforts by prisoners and outside groups to oppose and undermine Nazi control within the concentration camps, including acts of sabotage, escape attempts, and uprisings such as the Sonderkommando revolt.

Shoah: Another term for the Holocaust, derived from a Hebrew word meaning "catastrophe" or "destruction," used to describe the mass murder of six million Jews by the Nazis.

Sonderkommando: Jewish prisoners in Nazi death camps forced to work in the gas chambers and crematoria, aiding in the disposal of bodies.

SS (Schutzstaffel): A major paramilitary organization under Adolf Hitler and the Nazi Party, responsible for many of the crimes against humanity during the Holocaust, including the operation of concentration and extermination camps.

T4 Euthanasia Program: A Nazi policy of involuntary euthanasia that targeted disabled individuals and those deemed "unworthy of life."

Treblinka: Another Nazi extermination camp in occupied Poland, where more than 800,000 people were murdered. Like Auschwitz, it was part of the Nazi Final Solution.

Vichy France: The regime in France that collaborated with Nazi Germany after the country was occupied in 1940. The Vichy government participated in the persecution of Jews, including deportations to Auschwitz.

Wannsee Conference: A meeting held on January 20, 1942, where senior Nazi officials discussed and coordinated the implementation of the Final Solution, which led to the mass deportation and extermination of Jews in occupied Europe.

War Crimes: Serious violations of the laws and customs of war, including atrocities such as genocide, mass executions, and torture, many of which were prosecuted in the Nuremberg Trials following World War II.

Yad Vashem: The World Holocaust Remembrance Center in Jerusalem, Israel, dedicated to documenting the history of the Holocaust and preserving the memory of the victims.

Yellow Star: A badge that Jews were forced to wear in Nazi-occupied Europe, marking them for segregation, persecution, and eventual deportation to concentration camps.

Zyklon B: A cyanide-based pesticide used in the gas chambers of Nazi extermination camps to murder millions during the Holocaust.

BIBLIOGRAPHY

- Piper, Franciszek. "Auschwitz: How Many Perished Jews, Poles, Gypsies." Yad Vashem.
- Wiesel, Elie. *Night*. Hill and Wang, 1960.
- Kor, Eva Mozes, and Lisa Rojany Buccieri. *Surviving the Angel of Death: The Story of a Mengele Twin in Auschwitz*. Tanglewood, 2009.
- Perl, Gisella. *I Was a Doctor in Auschwitz*. International Universities Press, 1948.
- Hillesum, Etty. *An Interrupted Life: The Diaries of Etty Hillesum 1941-1943*. Pantheon Books, 1983.
- Frankl, Viktor E. *Man's Search for Meaning*. Beacon Press, 1959.
- United States Holocaust Memorial Museum. "Auschwitz: Inside the Nazi State." PBS, 2005.
- Levi, Primo. *If This Is a Man*. The Orion Press, 1959.
- Gilbert, Martin. *The Holocaust: A History of the Jews of Europe During the Second World War*. Holt, Rinehart and Winston, 1985.
- Gutman, Yisrael, and Michael Berenbaum, editors. *Anatomy of the Auschwitz Death Camp*. Indiana University Press, 1994.
- United States Holocaust Memorial Museum - Photo Courtesy
- Jewish Museum, Berlin.

ILLUSTRATIONS INDEX

- Display at Auschwitz I -Outdoor exhibit, showing a camp photo during winter - Page 5
- Display at Auschwitz I -Outdoor exhibit, showing women's barracks shortly after liberation - Page 6
- Display at Auschwitz I -Outdoor exhibit, featuring historical images of Auschwitz I - Page 7
- Display at Auschwitz I -Outdoor exhibit, showing historical photographs of children at Auschwitz - Page 8
- Entrance Gate to Auschwitz II-Birkenau - Page 13
- Auschwitz Territory, Summer 1944 - Page 22
- The Nuremberg Laws - Page 23
- Kraków Ghetto wall in Poland - Page 25
- Photographs of prisoners at Auschwitz II - Page 26
- Entrance gate of Auschwitz I with "Arbeit Macht Frei" sign - Page 27
- Entrance gate of Auschwitz I with "Arbeit Macht Frei" sign - Page 32
- Guard tower and warning sign at Auschwitz I - Page 33
- Pathways between brick barracks at Auschwitz I - Page 34
- Auschwitz I exterior with barbed wire fences and guard towers- Page 35
- Arrival of Jews from Hungry - Page 42
- Photographs of prisoners at Auschwitz I - Page 43
- Photograph of Used Zyklon B canisters - Page 50
- Photograph of entrance marked "DROGA ŚMIERCI" or "THE ROAD OF DEATH" - Page 51
- Camp Layout - Auschwitz 1 - Page 53
- Utensils used by prisoners - Page 60

- Abandoned luggage of prisoners - Page 61
- Reading glasses of prisoners - Page 62
- Prosthetic limbs and walking aids - Page 63
- Wall of Death at Auschwitz I, execution site - Page 64
- Guard tower at Auschwitz II-Birkenau - Page 65
- Camp Layout of Auschwitz II-Birkenau - Page 69
- Men's brick barracks at Auschwitz II-Birkenau - Page 71
- The photograph of the wooden freight car, used by the Nazis during the Holocaust - Page 72
- Remains of a gas chamber at Auschwitz II-Birkenau - Page 73
- Remains of a gas chamber at Auschwitz II-Birkenau - Page 80
- Remains of a gas chamber at Auschwitz II-Birkenau - Page 81
- Remains of a gas chamber at Auschwitz II-Birkenau - Page 82
- Interior of a crematorium at Auschwitz I - Page 83
- Interior of crematorium at Auschwitz I - Page 84
- The Chimney of a gas chamber at Auschwitz I - Page 85
- Interior of crematorium at Auschwitz I - Page 86
- Railway tracks leading into Auschwitz II-Birkenau - Page 87
- Entry from Anne Frank's Diary - Page 94
- Photograph of Oskar Schindler planting a tree - Page 97
- Photograph of a plaque installed at the Schindler's Factory in Kraków, Poland - Page 103
- Photograph of a mosaic of portraits at the Schindler's Factory in Kraków, Poland - Page 104
- Prisoners after liberated - Page 105
- Memorial Tablet at Auschwitz II-Birkenau- Page 110
- Photograph of barbed wire at Auschwitz II-Birkenau- Page 111
- The 'Piłsudski Bridge' in Kraków city - Page 115
- Execution Site at Auschwitz I - Page 116
- Solitary cattle car on railway tracks - Page 117
- A window from the Auschwitz-Birkenau State Museum - Page 124
- Crematorium and gas chamber complex at Auschwitz II-Birkenau- Page 125
- Female camp gate at Auschwitz II-Birkenau- Page 126

ACKNOWLEDGEMENT

I would like to express my deepest gratitude to those who made this book possible. To my parents, M. R. Dani and C. P. Dani, whose passion for travel and history ignited my own curiosity and love for exploring new places. Your guidance and shared adventures have been the foundation of my journey. To my sister, Nidhi Dani, whose unwavering support and encouragement have been a constant source of strength. Your belief in me and my work has inspired me to pursue my dreams with confidence.

To my wife Shivangi Kohli, and my son Iaan Dani, your love and patience have been my greatest strength throughout this journey. Your belief in me has kept me motivated and focused, and your presence has been a constant reminder of the importance of telling these stories.

To the survivors and their families, whose courage and resilience continue to inspire. To the historians and researchers, whose dedication to preserving the memory of Auschwitz-Birkenau ensures that the stories of those who suffered will never be forgotten. Special thanks again to my sister and my wife for their valuable feedback during editing and to everyone who has contributed to this project in any way. Your efforts are greatly appreciated.

ABOUT THE AUTHOR

I have poured countless hours and heartfelt thought into writing this book. As an avid traveler with a deep passion for history, this journey has been more than just documenting historical facts for me. It's about crafting an emotional experience that resonates with you. For me, writing transcends mere skill, it's a promise to ensure that the stories within these pages do not remain limited to the book but reach out and touch your soul. Witnessing the resilience of those who endured unimaginable hardships, the bravery of those who resisted, and the profound lessons ingrained in the very soil of these historic sites has left an indelible mark on me. I am moved by the strength of the human spirit and the vital lessons that places like Auschwitz impart. Through this book, I aim to bridge the past with the present, to emphasize the importance of remembrance, education, and the commitment needed to safeguard our future. As the author, my deepest hope is that these pages forge a connection with you. I aspire for this book to serve as a bridge, bringing you closer to the significance of memory, the necessity of education, and the dedication required to ensure our shared future is bright and just. My writing is a contribution to the ongoing conversation about our humanity.

Manit Dani

SCAN THE QR CODE
WITH YOUR CAMERA APP

Not working with your camera app?

Search for a free qr code reader on your app store.

Install the app and try scanning again.

Thank you for reading *The Last Ride: Journey to Auschwitz-Birkenau*. Your journey through these pages helps to keep the memory of those who lived through these events alive.

I would love to hear your thoughts. Connect with me on

Instagram: manitdani
Email: manitdani@gmail.com
Goodreads: Manit Dani

Your feedback is invaluable. Please consider leaving a review to share your reflections with others.